SUSAN ADAM

DOWN A PEG

A Book About Art & Culture
That Isn't Stuffy, Highbrow,
Reverential, Boring or Elitist

TABLE OF CONTENTS

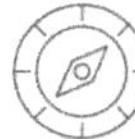

INTRODUCTION

DISCOVERING ART'S ROLE IN OUR DAILY LIVES

Fish discover water last - or so they say. This book is about that water (culture)
- the stuff in which we humans swim all day everyday.

Our environment is saturated with stories, images, fashion choices, music, social scripts, rituals and ceremonies - all indicators of the cultures operating around us. Being in a culture is like swimming with a school of fish - or riding the current. We are free to go in any direction but, instead, we choose to belong - to go with the flow. Life gets easier - most of the time.

This book is about one fish's experience discovering the water around her.

I hope you enjoy.

Here's how this journey began for me.

I remember the day in my bones. In the cells in my bones. November 22, 1963. I was a sophomore in high school sitting in Latin class. It was the first class after lunch. I was sitting in the second row from the door, second desk from the front. The loud speaker crackled on. And, in the next 30 seconds, the world changed for us all. Our president, John F. Kennedy, had been assassinated. Our Vice President, Lyndon Johnson, would soon be our president.

I was not a political kid. But I believed in Camelot. I had been raised with talk – no – IMAGES - of nuclear war. I dutifully tucked myself under my desk for drills – recognizing them as the useless exercises they were. I could imagine a bomb and I knew I would run two blocks north to the only family in the neighborhood with a bomb shelter – knowing full well that I would be turned away – and I would melt. I wondered what it would feel like to melt. Somehow that nightmare lived in the 'possibility' zone. But this? I watched my president with his Jackie – the couple who introduced a new way – who gave me a sense that Camelot was within reach. I watched them wave and smile. Then image after image of the bullet ... and the pink suit.

> "A single twig breaks, but the bundle of twigs is strong." –Tecumseh

Who does this? Something was forever lost for me that day. It's not that I was innocent, but ...

For the next few days, people were glued to their televisions – mourning together. Shops had their televisions on. People on benches listened to their radios. Stillness everywhere. A communal heartbroken stillness.

The grieving process changed everything for me. It showed me that cultures knew about these things (though I didn't know the word 'culture' at the time). They knew how to honor and console. They knew how to preserve stability in the midst of tragedy. They knew how to keep people together – tethered to one another - when everything else seemed lost.

Throughout it all I noticed the music. It was everywhere. Music that showed resolve and dignity – tenderness and tradition. There were choirs and soloists. Marine, Navy and Air Force bands. A Scottish pipe and drum regiment. A solo bugle. We heard Ave Maria, funeral marches, Hail to the Chief, America the Beautiful – and Taps. The seemingly endless sound of horses hooves and drums. Every note – every drumbeat – was experienced in communion with those around me – helping us all feel and process the truth together.

I witnessed rituals and symbolism. LBJ taking the oath of office. Vigils – everywhere. The flag draped casket. The horse-drawn caisson. Jet fighters in V formation – missing the last plane.

Air Force One dipping its wing. The riderless horse bearing reversed riding boots in thc stirrups. The 21-gun salute. The folding of the flag. Candles – and the eternal flame. And, the most poignant and heartbreaking image of them all - John-John saluting as his dad's remains passed by. Every one of these rituals was explained – in detail – as we all watched together.

I noticed how fashion had a hand in the ceremonies. Formal funeral attire. The black veil. The uniforms. The cardinals and bishops, priests and altar attendants. Scottish kilts. Black – just seas of black in every major city around the world as they congregated to honor and mourn. There was solidarity in the blackness of the moment and the attire. I was moved by how completely people followed the rules.

Although those days were crushingly sad, in some ways I was also heartened. I had seen what I didn't know was there. The power of cultures. We weren't alone.

I grew up in a lovely small town on the coast of Maine. A shipbuilding town. We were poor but lived on a street that was lined with glorious old sea captains' homes. Tucked down in behind (and below) those living museums, if you looked carefully, you would see a small house closer to the river. A house with a noisy chicken coop and a rambling garden. A smelting shanty and a few rusty cars were in the yard. That was my home - literally in the shadow of mansions.

The house immediately over mine was owned by an admiral and his wife, The Gilettes. One summer day, I had come up to street level and was headed north toward a friend's house. I was carrying my big tin of marbles. The Gilette's house was surrounded by a square granite fence – one thick enough for kids to mount as they walked that length of the sidewalk. As I walked by I saw two pale boys in the yard, blond hair, very white sneakers - wearing their shirts tucked into their shorts. I could immediately tell they were from 'away.'

As I walked by, the boys looked up and stopped what they were doing – staying back in the middle of the yard. I stopped and looked back at them. Petey waved – sort of – just lifting his hand without actually raising his arm. I smiled. After a couple of minutes they invited me to join them. I introduced them to the art and fun of marbles. The croakers. The cats eyes. Later, their mom called out from the porch, "Where are your manners, boys? Let's invite your new friend in. She can join us for dinner."

Over the next few hours I came to realize that what I had been told about how the world worked may not actually have been true.

The boys and their mom were visiting from New Orleans. Their accent alone tickled me. I wondered how they learned to talk that way – unaware that it was as natural to them as my Maine accent was to me. And going inside the house – well – I felt small. The ceilings were high. The staircase was like something out of a movie. The table – more glasses and silverware than there were people. And real napkins.

But the abundance I experienced was less about things and more about feeling seen and appreciated while I was there. They smiled at me – a lot. Even their eyes smiled. They asked me questions and listened.

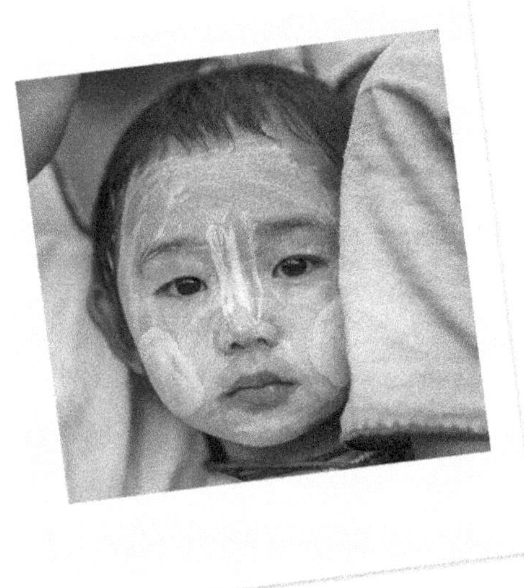

That was my introduction to Southern Hospitality. (Yes, I capitalized it.) And it threw my assumptions about class out the window. I never felt a hint of stuffiness or condescension even though I had been conditioned to do so.

Life back down in my house was very different. It was tiny with worn linoleum floors. We had a big oil stove that heated up the kitchen in winter and summer. At one point in his life my Dad had been successful - but all had been lost before I was born. I never knew him when he was riding high. The man I knew was tired and bitter. Rich people were the target of most of his insults. "They're not like us real people, Susie-Q. Be careful around them."

He was right. These people weren't like us. And I wanted to be like them. How did they get to be that way? You know, polite. Generous. Kind. I wanted to learn how to be polite – and generous – and kind.

I was an outsider. And I would feel like an outsider for most of my life. Belonging – well, feeling like I belonged - would take me a while. But, oh, what an interesting journey.

It's funny. Connecting with one another is natural. We are all hungry for it. It's like getting plugged into a bigger 'us.' But over millennia, as societies became more complex, so too did the expectations. Every culture and every group within a culture sets the rules. They draw the boundaries. They define in and out. Sometimes those boundaries are physical.

> "A child's education should begin at least one hundred years before he is born."
> –Oliver Wendell Holmes

When I was in sixth grade, we moved to the south part of town. Although Bath was a small town, this new neighborhood was decidedly more rural. Class time was easy for me. My former school had been way ahead in their curriculum – so I looked a bit like a know-it-all in this new group. Probably not the best way to begin. But recess time filled me with dread. No one reached out to invite me to join them. I awkwardly walked around the playground for a while – feeling all eyes on me. I sidled up to a group of other sixth grade girls – standing just a little outside the circle. Rachel, a tall girl with long brown hair, had all of their attention. She seemed older – and more experienced. She was talking about S-E-X. And I was totally lost. "He did this and I did this …" and all the other girls would gasp or giggle. I stood there oblivious – it was language I had not heard before. Mid-sentence, Rachel stopped and looked at me. "You don't get it, do you? What are you – some kind of baby?" I used my only practiced response – which was to smile. The circle closed with me on the outside. They migrated away.

They were right. I knew nothing. But I didn't understand why that disqualified me. I would later understand that there are some conversations meant for members only.

Growing up I watched – really watched – insiders and outsiders of all kinds. It was a survival strategy. Jocks, rich kids, cheerleaders, Mamma's boys and tomboys. Smart and nerdy kids and rebellious-hating-school kids. Each clique had its' own language, fashion, stories they told one another, musical preferences, heroes. They even carried themselves the same way. I learned how to read and respect that language. That belonging language. Little did I know that this knowledge would later serve as the cornerstone for my eventual love of the arts and all things fitting under the umbrella of 'culture.'

My art professors became inspirational guides in my life. They helped me see and long to know more. They turned me onto our human drive to build community. To connect to (and rely on) one another. I learned about the power of color and symbols. Cave paintings as carriers of ideas and spirituality. People experiencing real transcendence as they danced in circles around the fire. The rhythms. Stories and myths were conversations about goodness and strength – and an afterlife. People have forever used the arts to inspire, to communicate status or power, to express love or fear. To say, "See? I am like you," or "I am not like you."

This book is a culmination of a life lived in appreciation and wonder. Invitations to participate with our fellow earthlings are hiding in plain sight – all around us – every day. All it takes is a shift in our POV. We can recognize – and celebrate – fashion choices on passers-by for the stories they tell us. Or appreciate how the rituals of sports fans are manifestations of belonging. Or how stories about shared heroes serve as expressions of shared values. Whose faces adorn Inc. Magazine – or Glamour – or Sports Illustrated? Heroes all.

I consider myself an equal opportunity art appreciator. Of course there are masters who can change our lives with their creations. But for me there is wonderful expression in a lovingly done conventional quilt – or a handmade card – or a whimsical hairstyle choice. The amateur guitarist working day and night in order to meld into a small band. The keepers of flowerbeds. The wearers of "Have a nice day?" pins. The listeners. Visual, musical, fashion, storytelling expressions of connection. All weaving our cultures together.

> "We are all tattooed in our cradles with the beliefs of our tribe; the record may seem superficial, but it is indelible."
> –Oliver Wendell Holmes

We are all born into a constellation of people with their own beliefs and idiosyncrasies. We are born into a life already defined for us. Our communities invest in showing us the way. Their way. We learn these lessons through stories, images, traditions, the music played in our homes.

The longer I live, the more I understand – and appreciate – that the starter kits we are given at birth will always be with us. They are ours to carry throughout our lives. We can choose to live differently, or to believe differently, but our beginnings will revisit us throughout our journey.

Why this book? Why now? We are in a period of true cultural stress. Let's face it, outrage seems to be the position of choice for too many of us. "They" are wrong. "It's us against them." I feel it and I'll bet you've experienced a round or two of it yourself. The differences are there – and true – and important.

But so are our connections. We all love music – just different music. We all love stories – but just with different heroes. And we all get stuck behind our masks and just want to laugh at our own ridiculousness.

So I offer you some stories, some looks into how the arts are at work in our daily lives. I share personal stories hoping you see yourselves reflected in them too.

> "(Art) is part of what distinguishes what it is to be human from other life forms on Earth – that we have culture."
> –Neil deGrasse Tyson

I begin by focusing on five core art 'disciplines' – a chapter for each. We'll explore how we use our APPEARANCE as social radar – helping us find like-minded people. Or the science and beauty of MUSIC as it tangles itself into our emerging identity. In THEATER & ACTING we explore how we learn our lines – how we try on roles – as we become the people we aspire to be. STORYTELLING gives us myths, fairy tales, history and even the daily news. When we dig into VISUAL ART, we explore the power of images and symbols to make us feel – and take action. Chapter-hopping is fine – they aren't in sequence. I close each of these chapters with some suggestions on how to engage children in this exploration.

My final chapter, as you might expect, is IN PRAISE OF ARTISTS in our lives. I'm all verklempt at the thought of it. Although we almost never meet them, we know them. Intimately. We feel connected to them because they share themselves courageously and honestly. It's what they do. They may be shy as hell and yet they trust us with the truth. They wake up our emotions and help us feel in communion with one another.

I hope you enjoy what you read – and I hope you enjoy what you perhaps rediscover in your own lives.

CHAPTER 1

VISUAL ARTS IN OUR LIVES

"My art is about paying attention – about the extremely dangerous possibility that you might be art." – Robert Rauschenberg

First, some facts … What happens inside you when you see a swastika? It isn't like a crescent and star or a cross that represents a belief system. Or a rose that represents looooove. Or a mermaid who represents – what is it – oh yeah – a coffee brand. No, it is so much bigger than that. And darker than that.

That symbol warns us of what we humans are capable of if we lose our way, conjuring up an entire culture so filled with hate and vengeance that it could starve and kill millions of Jews with detachment and efficiency. And it's a symbol that has power - still. It threatens and intimidates today like an aftershock of an old horror.

And yet it is a simple graphic image. People gave it meaning. People gave it power.

Deep cleansing breath.

We absorb images 30 times faster than the blink of an eye. Think of that. As long as our eyes are open we are taking in information – and making sense of it. It is not just, "Isn't that beautiful!" or "I'm not sure green works on that wall." It's more like, "Do I know and can I trust this person?" "Is that fruit ripe?" "Where is the exit?" In that blink of an eye incoming data splits into two directions - with most going to our visual cortex (what we would expect – quickly putting the pieces together into images so we don't bump into those walls) and some of that information going directly to our hypothalamus gland.

That's right – a gland that has nothing to do with forming images. Instead it plays a crucial role in many of our bodily functions like regulating our emotional responses, releasing hormones, controlling our appetites, regulating our body's temperature – even managing our sexual behavior. Mother Nature knew we might only have that fraction of a second to react if what we see is danger, so she kept a direct route to our fight or flight response just in case. This area can defy logic. There wouldn't be time for logic. And then in the next split second – more images to process ... and the next.

> "To photograph is to frame, and to frame is to exclude." –
> Susan Sontag

Even things in the background – things that don't reach our consciousness – get seen and filed and can influence us.

Colors, just pure colors, can affect our moods, our appetites, our memory. No image necessary. Just color. Subconsciously.

The world is filled with expressions of identity. With a glance we can recognize symbols of power and authority, school busses, team logos, churches and synagogues. We know a Navajo blanket from an Amish quilt – and what they mean. We can tell the wealth of a person, their gender, race and maybe their faith. In a blink. We have to see fast. Photographs, in an instant, flash images that provoke our mirror cells to feel compassion – or to yearn for a burger. One look

at the contortions in Guernica and we feel the costs of war. Walking through a Japanese garden weaves esthetics and philosophy together in the moment. And standing inside in the afternoon light of Gaudi's Sagrada Familia – well – I simply don't have words for that feeling. Art can go straight for our primitive heart-thumping, vulnerable self - bypassing thought in the blink of an eye.

Our homes, too, are saturated with visual stories that mean something. Probably something dear to us. The patterns of plates and pillows and carpets all carefully chosen because somehow they spoke to us – or speak for us. If we unexpectedly see the wallpaper pattern of our childhood, we can be overwhelmed with feelings of nostalgia. A simple throw pillow, appearing to be tossed randomly, is actually placed. It matters to us. So many of our surroundings have nothing to do with utility or efficiency. They are there because it feels good to have them there. They connect us to our families and memories and heritage. They inspire and calm us down. Our homes are like visual wombs – setting us apart from the outside world.

SYMBOLS

Symbolism brings meaning and emotional value to the things we do and use every day. The peace sign. A salute. The sign of the cross. Wedding rings. Handshakes. Doves. Raising your right hand. Four leaf clovers. Scouts crossing over. We humans find endless ways to bring meaning – no – to SHOW meaning – in our daily lives.

Just two days after 9/11, those of us who lived below 14th Street in NYC were allowed to return to our homes. I lived on Broadway and 12th. All day every day I watched truck after truck pass by my window carrying the shards of the World Trade Center buildings. I walked to the site before it was cordoned off and found everything covered with heavy ash. As traumatizing as that was, it got harder. Everywhere – on every building and every bus stop and every tree – there were pictures of missing mothers, fathers, daughters and sons. People – now gone. Everywhere. Hospitals had been ready on that day – but no one came. We were realizing it was worse - much worse - than we could have possibly imagined.

On the third night, in Union Square, people gathered for a vigil supported by the Gay Men's Chorus. The organizers greeted us from every direction, giving us each a candle – and a welcome. When the hymns began and the flame was passed from one to another to another – it was something greater than a prayer. Our souls – our spirits – were finding one another. The simple gesture of sharing the light of a candle bypassed our thinking brains and all that we knew to be true - and brought us into communion with one another. I felt myself exhale for the first time in days. A feeling of returning home. The candles knit us together.

Of course candles don't knit. And peace signs don't bring peace. And flags don't defend us. But they all speak a language beyond logic that goes straight to what it means to be human - a language rooted in the arts.

> "A symbol serves to combine heart and intellect."
> —Robert Penn Warren

The voices of the singers consoled and held us tight. There was tragedy at our doorsteps and yet - here we were. Alive. After the hymns a very brief pause and then - "These little town blues ..."

We were in good hands. Very good hands.

PINK AND BLUE

Let's say you are at the mall – perhaps getting a coffee - when you see an acquaintance carrying a baby in a Baby Bjorn. Suddenly you remember seeing an announcement a month or so earlier but, for the life of you, you can't remember – was it a boy or a girl? You look for any giveaways. Is there a pink ribbon clipped onto that thin hair? Is there a blue puppy insignia? Quick. Gotta find something. The mom looks at you while gently patting the baby's bottom.

After a quick hug and greeting, you bite the bullet and ask, "Is it a boy or a girl?"

You needed to know because … well, because you had work to do. From the minute we know a baby's sex, we have cultural scripts ready to go. A boy? We lower our voices a bit – perhaps use the words 'buddy' and 'handsome' or 'good-looking.' A girl? A higher voice with words like 'sweetie' and 'honey.'

All adults in a culture, not just parents, work together to ensure that the next generation is ready for their turn on stage. We want kids to be accepted so they, too, can be safe. We do it out of love. We play a little rougher with our toddler boys and give baby dolls to little girls.

Starting assumptions are important and can be beautiful. But too often we forget that those starting assumptions are arbitrary. They change over time. They must change over time so we prepare our kids for their world.

So – the pink and blue caps on newborns in hospital nurseries aren't for the babies. They are our cue. Our starting gate – and we're off to the races readying the next generation.

WE EAT FIRST WITH OUR EYES

Okay. I'll admit it. It is just a dite self-indulgent. Being an unattached 'senior' woman, I long ago made peace with the fact that we have only one life to live. NOT dining out because I am solo – well – that has always been out of the question. I will repeat. We have only one life to live. Maybe that's why the experience of savoring is a bit more intense. This is not a social experience first, enhanced by the food. Nooooo. This is about the food.

The menu said, 'Fiori di Carciofi' – artichoke, mint oil and crispy garlic chips. Nothing to argue with there, right? But when it came, there before me was this work of art. A perfect blossom - like a spiraling shell holding its pale green contents – sitting in a golden glistening buttery broth flecked through with bits of fresh mint. Sprinkled atop this perfection were lots of dark amber crispy garlic chips – curly compliments. All presented in a pristine white bowl.

> "As long as autumn lasts, I shall not have hands, canvas and colors enough to paint the beautiful things I see."
> –Vincent Van Gogh

I mentioned that I was dining alone. It was probably a good thing at that moment. Conversation would have been stilted to say the least with that bundle of distraction in front of me. Of course I savored – a bit of reverence for the heights we people can achieve. Appreciation. Then – another bite. And a sip of that carefully selected wine. If anyone doubts the art in that experience – well - you and me, we have to talk.

This is performance art as much as it is culinary and visual. All of our senses are involved: the ambiance and excitement of the restaurant itself; the aromas; the linens and stemware; and, of course, the taste. But the presentation on the plate introduces the stars of the show. I wish applause was customary when a piece of perfection is set down before us. I would excitedly say to all the other patrons, "Hey. Look at this. Can you see this? Isn't it wonderful?" But instead I will try my best to look - refined.

My mother-in-law came from a place filled with culture and finesse and traditions. Plus a place of war and pain. She was from East Germany. She actually worked in the first Volkswagen plant. For you history buffs, yes, that was under Hitler. After a perilous journey to the US with her husband and son, my Frankie, she learned the language and adapted to our culture. To a certain point.

Of course immigrants want to hold onto their old ways. Those old ways are part of their identity. They are important — and beautiful. And, of course, they want to participate in their new culture. Everyone draws that line in a different place.

For Annemarie, she drew the line at dinnertime. Any meal, actually. Anytime we gathered around the table it was like stepping back into old Europe. China, silver and crystal at every meal. There were proper ways to present food. To serve food. The details on the china and the teacups were clearly from another era. Each cup and saucer was unique — and completely perfect. The lace tablecloths. The place settings. Perfect. The wursts needed one kind of plate. The tartare another.

And her butter roses. Oh my! I learned how to make a decent butter rose. It became part of the fun and formality of our Thanksgiving dinners. That is, until people discovered salads. Now my butter roses rarely see the light of day — and when they do they are often untouched. Good as new at the end of the meal.

Paying attention to all the details — the visual stories — is a way of bringing focus to the real importance of the meal. Of dining together. These details say it matters that we are together at this moment. Frankie's family was not wealthy. They held onto a few precious pieces of tradition — and filled in the rest.

Perhaps that's the thing about mothers-in-law. Their version of the-way-things-are-done – their cultural roots - almost always differ from our own. But, I have to say that very difference offers us a chance to see ourselves in a new light – to articulate why our way means something to us.

So – a few decades later I, too, have a collection of precious teacups. When my granddaughter was eight we began our tea parties – carefully picking out the designs we wanted each time. Relishing the history and ceremony we held in our hands. And, not to be corny – but in our hearts as well.

THE SPIRIT IN THINGS

A survey was conducted by the City University of New York asking people, "If the Mona Lisa was destroyed in a fire, which would you rather see? A perfect replica of the masterpiece or the ashes of the original? Eighty percent of respondents chose the ashes of the Mona Lisa.

It wasn't even a close call, was it? What does that tell us?

When we see IT – when we stand in front of that Picasso or Kahlo or Rembrandt – it is about so much more than the paint. Sure we can lean in and see the strokes. But there is something else – something magic - afoot. Do you have any items in your home crafted or used by someone dear to you? That toddler chair built by grandpa. The recipes in your mother's hand. Perhaps a serving platter handed down for generations. It is not about the retail value of these things. What makes these things priceless is the sense that the creator's contact with the object – their attention and love – somehow becomes an intrinsic part of them. Their spirit touches us when we hold them. Or when we stand in front of them at a museum.

Our surroundings are alive in many ways. The rocking chair bursts with memories. Old bowls or utensils handed down – or bought at a flea market – have life attached to them. We hold what someone else held. It matters. The experience is not about logic but about connection. We see that we touch this earth and leave something behind for others.

I have a pink chenille crib blanket that was mine when I was a baby. When I see that on the next generation – and the next – well, the full story of life comes to mind, does it not? Providing comfort once more. Perhaps there should be an 'Antiques Roadshow' equivalent – called 'What This Means to Me Roadshow.'

DO YOU SEE WHAT I SEE? NO.

I would announce to the employees seated around me for the MBTI workshop that I would be walking around the room displaying an image. They'd all get approximately 10 seconds of viewing time. They would then be asked to jot down what they saw.

Sounds pretty simple, right? When asked to read only what they had written down, the majority usually responded with: it is night; a mountain to the left; four cars on the road near the top and a few near the bottom; seven or eight tall contemporary buildings all lit up – looking like they were a half mile away. Etc. Details.

And there was always another group – usually 25 – 30% - who would describe the scene this way: Looks like a storm just passed. There is electricity in the air. Dampness. Ominous.

"Your home should tell the story of who you are." –Nate Burkus

Same picture. All true. Some noticed the details (the trees) and others noticed patterns and big picture (the forest).

I found the Myers Briggs Type Indicator (MBTI) to be very useful in organizations. It was always an employee favorite because it gave people language to understand themselves and others – often step number one when you're trying to create a positive employee culture. The exercise I described was used to demonstrate that we process incoming information differently; we either prefer noticing the trees first (S) or the big picture and trends first (N). No preference is better than the other. We can all do everything. We tend to get better at our preferred processes because we use them more often.

So – what does this have to do with visual arts? Particularly visual arts in our daily lives? We can look at a newly renovated room – or a painting – or a movie – and leave with two different stories to tell. I have always had a strong preference for big picture and patterns. My friend, Yvonne, had an opposite preference, strongly leaning toward details. One day we were walking down Fifth Avenue just south of Rockefeller Center – so – a tourist-rich area. In areas like Wall Street where we would find primarily 'experienced sidewalk-walkers,' people keep moving. No solid walls of people walking four abreast. They wouldn't do that. Instead you see quick shifts and rivulets opening up all the time. People managing to flow through one another.

But this was Fifth Avenue on a Saturday and movement was slow. Not only do tourists walk four abreast, but they chat – and point – and stop, oblivious to the people all around them shifting their weight from side to side ready for any hint of an opening. On this sunny day I was taking it all in – trying to look beyond the current obstruction to see which side I should dive for - when Yvonne grabbed my arm and said, "Man, did you see the ring on that woman!"

At the end of this day – although we were in the same time and place - we saw entirely different stories?

LET'S HEAR IT FOR THE SMILEY FACE EMOJI!

Wait! Come back! I know you couldn't see my body language when I said that. All you could see were the words. Come back and I'll explain.

Did you know that when we communicate with one another face-to-face, ninety-three percent of how the message is interpreted comes from the nonverbal elements? Only seven percent comes from the words themselves.

Okay – I'll give you a minute to reflect on all the text messaging and emails in our lives.

Words. Just lots of words. We can't hear the person's tone. Are they laughing? Shrugging their shoulders? Placing their hand on their hearts? Whispering? … Smiling?

The simple ubiquitous smiley emoji has given us a way to say something - perhaps not the most profound something - but something still very true. It communicates about our mental state or our reaction. That gesture – those thanks – that news – whatever precedes it has been received, consumed and is appreciated. Thumbs up emoji.

Though we are rarely aware of it, we humans automatically mimic each other's expressions, emotions and even body language. It's an important part of any conversation. It's one of the ways Mother Nature helps us connect and build communities. But when we are online – well – that doesn't happen, does it? It's like understanding one word in ten. We don't get the full message.

Scientists have discovered that when we see an online smiley face, the same parts of the brain are activated as when we see a real human face. Our mood changes and sometimes our faces change too – into a smile – just as if there was a smiling person in front of us.

Maybe emojis only get us to the fifty-yard line – but that's a whole lot better than the seven-yard line, don't you think? Pondering emoji.

SAY CHEESE – NO, SHOW ME A PICTURE OF CHEESE

We have a remarkable ability to remember pictures. Research has shown that people can remember more than 2,000 pictures with 90% accuracy over a period of several days. Words and text? Well, the story is not so good. We remember only 10% of what we read a mere three days later. I'll check in with you in three days to test those percentages.

Combine that same text with a related image and – bingo - we can remember 65% of the information three days later. That phenomenon is the Picture Superiority Effect.

But remembering is just the tip of the iceberg. Recent research has shown how even the subtlest elements in a photo can have profound effects on us. In one experiment, toddlers were shown one of two pictures. Both had the same interesting activity in the foreground and in the background stood a standard bookcase. On that bookcase, there would either be (1) a small framed photo of two people happily facing one another, obviously cooperating - OR (2) a small framed photo of two people turned away from one another, looking uncooperative. Other than that small detail, the pictures were identical.

After the toddlers got a quick exposure to the photo, an adult would walk into the room, stumble, and spill their box of toys. Those children shown the first photo (cooperation) were way more likely to help the researcher pick up spilled toys than those who had seen photo #2. It happened instantly and automatically.

Just seeing cooperation immediately prior to the slip made the children more likely to be cooperative.

When I read that, I was suddenly tempted to put pictures of cooperation in front of every member of congress. We humans are born to align – to mimic – what we see in others.

THE DAY I MET PABLO PICASSO –
OKAY, I DIDN'T ACTUALLY MEET PABLO PICASSO

But he knew me. He knew what I needed more than I knew what I needed. He looked into my eyes and said, "Susan. What are you doing? Get out of that comfy chair – and comfy role (okay, I'm sure he wouldn't use the word comfy) and get ready to see some truth. There is so much more going on in life under the surface if you just look with new eyes. If you just …. jump." On the way home from 'meeting' him so many of my assumptions had been unraveled that I actually felt a little beat up. Within a couple of years – when both kids were safely off to college - I was doing a trust fall into the universe. I jumped. I moved to New York City without a job.

Meeting Picasso. It was 1980. Three Maine teacher friends and I packed ourselves into a vintage Volvo and made the trip to the Picasso Retrospective at the Museum of Modern Art. It was my first trip to New York City. I returned home a different person.

Of course I was familiar with his work – or so I thought. But to see what he could do at twelve years old – and fifteen years old – to see how bored he must have been just doing what other artists worked a lifetime to master. Then – to see the cracks – the ways he began to test us viewers. If a figure has four sides, who says we can't contemplate all four sides at once? It's a painting – not a photo. We got to consider things that we knew to be true captured in new ways. Gallery after gallery of him saying to me, "Susan, try to keep up." I loved that he had high expectations of me. I had to work to get a smile out of him.

We'd round a corner and, of course, a whole new palette of ideas and techniques. And then another. Sometimes it felt like he was shouting. Or pulling my leg. Or just plain showing off. And then - Guernica.

Here we got to see, not just the completed work, but also his work process. Around the huge masterpiece the museum had mounted several of his detailed studies – particularly of that gut-wrenching horse. Suddenly I felt like I was looking over his shoulder – seeing how hard he really worked on every single element. No brash spontaneity here. Just carefully rendered elements meant to pack a punch. To show war for what it was.

> "Painting is not done to decorate apartments. It is an instrument of war."
> –Pablo Picasso

Picasso had said, "If I paint a wild horse, you might not see the horse … but surely you will see the wildness." Guernica showed us the pain of war like no other.

Different artists speak to different people. Sometimes their visions and intentions come to us unexpectedly. If we are lucky, we can take a pause and listen.

Sometime I'll tell you about Toulouse-Lautrec and me. It's about how he can show the softness of aging flesh with just a line. It's a love story. But that's a story for another day.

BRINGING THE CONVERSATION ABOUT
VISUAL ARTS TO CHILDREN

Toy manufacturers have outdone themselves with all those big bright plastic shapes and colors. I suspect that, long before children can speak, they are bored with the garish simplicity of them all. Children are born with a capacity and appetite for nuance, detail and patterns. Let's feed that hunger. Let's encourage paying attention to the beautiful complexity in their lives. Let's help them read and understand all the messaging that surrounds them.

NOTICE! EVERYTHING!

While driving, encourage your child to see with curiosity. Help them see deeply rather than quickly.

Notice buildings during the day and at night – how the light changes the geometry. Notice how colors change at dusk. Notice the color of cars in traffic. Notice store fronts. Notice residential neighborhoods where the houses all look the same. Talk about zoning rules and how communities control 'the look' of the world around them. Notice landscaping. Explore why some use a rigid code and others look more on the wild side. You get the 'picture.'

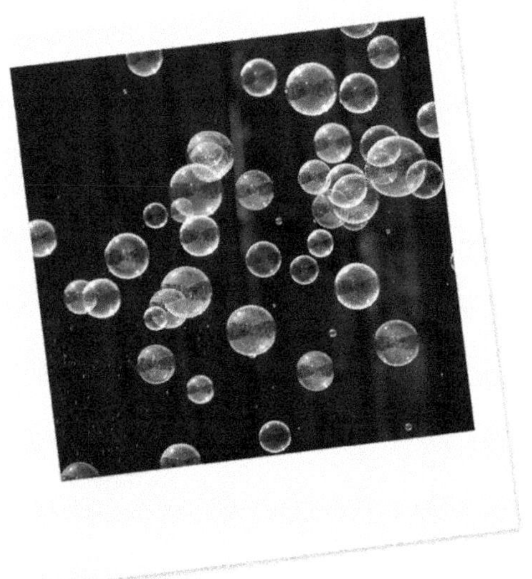

"Why do you think some colors are more popular than others?

Why do you think the community installed specific sculptures in the park? Why would that matter to people?

Why might people want different styles?

Stop and Yield signs - why do they all need to look the same?

THE WONDER OF SYMMETRY

This conversation can build your child's awareness of the power of balance and symmetry in their lives. They will see that it is everywhere in their world. So much in nature grows symmetrically. Leaves and trees. Lobsters and mice. Antlers and sea shells. You and me.

Start noticing houses with centered doors and symmetrical windows. Haircuts. Pictures hung on walls. Those things on the mantel. Table settings. Cabinets. Curtains. Pillows on the sofa. Dibs on who spots something symmetrical first.

WHAT DO YOU SEE FIRST?

This conversation can build your child's awareness of how artists and designers can influence where our eyes go, making sure we get the main message. The super-red lipstick. The eyes. The neon signs. Eventually your child will be able to use those concepts in their own lives.

Create a habit (not annoyingly frequent) of stopping action and asking, "What do you see first?" when you enter a room or a home for the first time.

Book covers. Cereal boxes. Billboards. When they look in a mirror ...

OH, THAT HOME SPRITE IS AT IT AGAIN!

These activities can help keep your young child aware of their home environment. When things remain the same, they can become invisible. When you mix it up they will 'see' it again. And see things in a new way. Surprises delight. Have fun being surprised with them – "Oh that mischievous sprite was at it again." Your child will notice – even if you never mention it.

Try mixing up how you normally stack towels and sheets.
Alternate colors? Stack in blocks? Roll them up?

Are the things on your coffee table needing a shuffle? Turn some things upside down.

Have a big comfy chair face the wall.

Remove a framed picture from the wall – and hang – a child's sweater – or a hat.

Instead of throw pillows on either end of the sofa, try piling them in the middle.

While they are at school, make their beds the opposite way – with the head where the feet used to be.

Turn a mirror around. Set the table with silverware facing sideways.

IMAGES AND SYMBOLS CAN PACK A PUNCH

Help them appreciate that images represent something important and intangible to them.

Discuss a photo they have that is important to them. How would they feel if someone set a glass of water on it - or threw it on the floor?

Explore a few flags and symbols in your child's life – national – or a banner from your faith – or a favorite sports team. Why do you think people carry, fly or wear them? Desecrating them can offend - or even threaten.

WHO IS THE BOSS OF ART?

The arts are so powerful that some dictators fear them. They know the arts can change people's feelings and even make them feel empowered to make a change in their government.

What might happen if people living under a dictator wore t-shirts that were insulting to the dictator?

Do you think it takes courage to write and perform songs that criticize leaders in free countries? In dictatorships?

How do you think other citizens feel or react when they see risky art?

Let's try to find art in our country that might not be legal under a dictatorship.

The purpose of these discussions is to help your child notice all the visual messaging in their environments. So many brands promise to help people show 'coolness,' belonging and individuality. Using brands as personal identifiers can seem like an easy solution to social challenges. Bottom line – it is important to understand that these logos are marketing – meant to sell.

> *What do you think of the (a current, trendy) logo?*
>
> *If you had two identical pairs of sneakers, but only one had the logo on it, which one would you choose? Why?*
>
> *If some brands are more expensive, does wearing them tell the world about the wearer's financial status? Why might that matter? What if your family can't afford them?*

CHAPTER 2

POWER OF MUSIC IN OUR LIVES

A song can steal upon you in the dark, on a road, far from home, blow out your tires and leave you sobbing, in gratitude, at the wheel." –Wyatt Mason, New York Times Magazine

First, some facts … Categorizing music as entertainment is like saying the ocean is wet. It kinda misses the point, doesn't it? There is way more to the story. We are musical creatures. It is like a rising tide inside us, making everything inside more fluid and connected. Our feelings are aroused and calmed. Our memories flash forward as if they happened yesterday. The impulse to move – to sway, to tap – to dance – is almost irresistible. It's us with our lights on. Even with no external music, we sing inside.

Our physical and emotional reactions to harmony and dissonance are being studied like giant math challenges. Listening to (and relistening to) sad songs can be 3-minute journeys into our feelings – to mingle and linger with them – healing at our own pace. Music defines cultures and generations. And love. Is love even possible without music? "I hear singing and there's no one there. ... You're not sick. You're just in love."

Music is central to human development and connection. Moving together is a life-long bonding activity. It begins in the womb. Anyone trying to comfort a baby knows how a rhythm change – or a bounce instead of a sway – can make a difference. Babies respond to even the subtlest changes in tempo. It's a language they already understand. From lullabies to love songs to anthems and hymns. From music that makes our bodies move with power and joy – to violins that touch us so deeply we cry. We just cry. We communicate with one another – we merge with one another.

Music is a pharmacy. Stressed or anxious? High blood pressure? Need help grieving? Low in energy? Surgeons find that music reduces pre-surgery anxiety in patients. And surgical teams? Well music is almost universally used in the operating room to promote focus and teamwork.

And those who were seen dancing were thought to be insane by those who could not hear. –Friedrich Nietzsche

So – entertainment? Yes, but .....!!! Let's explore a few of the ways we all find this art form active – bossy, actually – in our daily lives.

THE DANCE

Picture this. We are with friends at a busy nightclub enjoying our favorite cocktails. There is a small dance floor. Or we are at a wedding with a glass of champagne. Or at a street fair with our macchiato - when the band starts to play. It doesn't matter if the music is live – or if there is a crowd – or if we are dressed up or dressed down. That will all disappear soon enough. The warm front is moving in.

The music begins - perhaps with a slight Latin rhythm. It's already too late. The music is now in control. I notice someone else who is also feeling the rhythm. Nothing over-the-top, mind you. He can be my age. 20 years older. Or 20 years younger. It doesn't matter. It's not about that. I once danced with Slim, a bearded man 30 years my senior at a country and western bar in Washington DC and he took me to school. The eyes gesture toward the dance floor. The hand is extended. Consent is given. We are stepping into the ring.

We walk side-by-side to the floor already moving in sync, then turn to one another. Nothing is said as I put my arm over his shoulder. He leans in as he puts his hand low on my back. Eye contact. Smiles. Any colognes or hints of shampoo add to the magic. Everything else becomes background.

Music provides the time/space arena where we meet and move as one. We slowly get to know and match each other's energy. Face to face. With each turn we understand each other better. We encourage or lean into or match one another. The whole time this music – this hypnotic, pulsing force – seems to burst from inside us rather than as an outside force. Our heartbeats are aligned. Our breathing is aligned.

Our bodies have wanted to do this all along. The windsock man in us is free. And then, unlike other forms of (uh) intimacy, we can do it again.

I don't know about you, but I need a glass of water.

Moving together to music is an impulse – an integrated response – that is hardwired into our nature. Our brains and our bodies come fully loaded. It's the culmination of eons of evolution designed to make us powerful and safe through our connections to one another. Science tells us that when we dance together, particularly if we are synchronized in our movements, the boundaries between me and 'we' fade. We can't quite tell where we end and the other person begins.

Relief. Connection.

Our favorite musical group is coming to town. We post our tickets on the refrigerator – a daily boost of anticipation. Of course, we plan everything so we can be there early – and ready. This is important – vital, even. We know it's not just about the music – or the brush with celebrities. We love this band or performer for a reason. They have spoken for us – and to us. Or pulled us through. They tapped into our needs or our rage or our loneliness – our longing for love. Their songs were like magnets with our friends – shared enthusiasm without ever having to discuss our individual pain. It's all assumed when we find a group we all love.

> **Rock and roll itself can be described as music to accompany the rite of passage. – Pete Townshend**

The lights go down. The audience is like a jumpy racehorse at the gate. We can feel the energy. Then the first chords – those familiar meaningful chords - blast through us at full volume reaching not only our ears but rattling inside our chests. Like lightening reaching everyone in the audience at the same time.

At this point – and throughout the concert – we become one. We move – together. We cheer – together. We can no longer hear our own voices because we are part of a bigger whole. Our heart beats and our breathing align. The parts of our brains controlling empathy – light up. We scream – from the deepest parts of our lonely souls - because we can. Because we feel those deep deep feelings. We feel that human condition – together.

Stomp – stomp – clap! Stomp – stomp – clap! Stomp – stomp – clap!

I liken a good screaming concert to a shiatsu massage – releasing all those toxins. We leave feeling a little bruised – but looser. Lighter.

EMOTIONAL MASSAGE

We all experience those times in our lives when life hands us something that we need to deal with. The kinds of things that we put on the back burner when at work – or in front of the kids. It might be some kind of loss. Or when faced with a consequential decision. For me, its time to get into the car, roll up all the windows, and play those songs that take me into my own heart. I visit with the sadness or regret or fear. I may cry with it. Or sing with it. And then the key changes and I am on my way back up to the surface. Safely. And then I play it again – and again – until I am done.

There are voices that touch us. Or melodies. Or harmonies. Or instrumentation. Cellos – oboes – well, they understand how much I hurt. They linger. No hurrying. Sometimes just feeling understood is enough. When I play Yo-Yo Ma's *Ave Maria* – I honestly hear the hand reaching out to me – to comfort me as the song begins. It invites me into the experience of solace and comfort. Every single time. Even if I am on top of the world, when that song comes on, I accept the invitation. It adds to the sweetness of the day.

MUSIC IS THERE FOR TEENS TOO

Kids face hard times. So much is on the line for them. There aren't many of us who would voluntarily repeat our teen years. Thank goodness, once again, music is there - providing scaffolding for understanding themselves and their world.

Angelina was a good, but troubled, teen. Smart. Kind. Torn apart by a mother struggling with her own demons. She turned to cutting. And she turned to music. Those of us who loved her were worried that the music she was listening to was part of the problem. Here is some of my interview with her. Let's just say she took me to church.

Why do you think those types of music appeal to you?

"So many of the lyrics are just easy to relate to. Kurt Cobain, the kind of image he displayed – the whole suicide thing. He's been where you are – feeling overwhelmed just like so many of us. It's not unhealthy to appreciate someone who ultimately killed himself. That's not why I like him. I appreciate him because he was able to expose the pain, to capture what it feels like. So he is a hero in that way.

When you listen to different artists, over time you build relationships with them, like friends. Lyrics and melody are like a bridge to where you are. Whenever I'm in my best state of mind or worst state of mind, music is there for me. I'm connected."

I'd like to speak as a parent for a minute. We do our best to understand and want to protect you, so we just naturally worry that the music you are drawn to might bring you down even further. That it can trigger depression. Can you understand that?

> They're powerful, those songs. At times they've been my only way back, the only door out of the dark, bad places the black dog calls home. –Johnny Cash

"Please trust me and my music! I don't listen to songs that make me feel worse. No one does. I want to feel better and it begins by seeing that others have felt the same way. Even if parents don't understand why we feel frustrated, those are our feelings. By digging into the emotions and giving them room, I come to understand them better. Then I can get to a different emotional plane.

Music reflects universal feelings. It doesn't come and go, whereas friends move on. Music is like a band-aid that is always there for you."

She said it well. Sad music doesn't make us sad. It's just there with us.

MUSIC MAKES HARD WORK EASIER AND EASY WORK FUN

Do you have a yard that needs tending? A kitchen to clean? A dog to walk? Again? Music puts the chore in its place – as background. "Calgon, take me away," an 80's ad for bath salts, pretty much says it all. The music takes us away. Although there may be a mop or leash in our hands, our minds can go where they need, or want, to go. Science has shown that music activates nearly every region of our brain that's been mapped so far. With the ease of a slip 'n slide, old memories come to life, emotions rush in, we can see problems in new ways.

But – take heed. It can be easy to forget where you are. One day I was clearing leaves while listening to, as one does, *Mambo #5*. The Lou Bega version.   I started raking with, let's just say, a little style. And then, it wasn't about the leaves at all. Who knew that rakes make great mambo partners! It was only when I saw a neighbor standing in her driveway – just watching me that I 'came to.' "Hello. Nothing to see here. Just raking."

DA-DUM - MUSIC CARRIES THE EMOTIONAL LOAD IN MOVIES

I grew up on the Maine coast so I had lots of happy beach time with my kids. I can remember everything about that night sitting in our car at the drive-in theater. The first feature – a Disney movie - was over. It was 9:30ish and the kids had fallen asleep in the backseat which had been turned into a big comfy bed. I don't know what I was expecting – heck – it was a movie about a shark – so of course it would be scary. A little scary. But, this?!? Scenes of water – and kids playing – and that bone-chilling unstoppable theme. We didn't see the shark. We didn't need to see the shark. The deepest fear and dread overcame me.

There is art and science behind it all. We may be aware that we are watching a fictional story, but those feelings are real. Our hearts beat faster. We feel true fear or true sadness. And those feelings connect us to the characters and to all the people around us.

We are musical creatures by nature. When we hear it, there is almost no barrier or speed bump. We get shivers with a crescendo. While our eyes and our brains are focused on the screen, the score has free reign to take us on the emotional ride.

If you want a peek into this undercurrent, watch a show with subtitles. I recently watched The Confession - a multi-part British series about a real-life police officer searching for victims. I had subtitles activated, so the musical descriptions were displayed along with the dialogue. Here is the actual musical storyline for just a few minutes while the characters were driving through the countryside on their way to a potential burial site.

"Dark ambient music - suspenseful music - birds singing - tense music - children laughing - dramatic music - engine revving - tense music - melancholy music - phone ringing - somber music - swelling with dramatic music - helicopter whirs - breathes heavily - helicopter whirs - birds singing - eerie ominous music …"

Since I was able to actually hear the music I was seeing described, I started getting a sense of the subtle differences between suspenseful and ominous – and between somber and melancholy. But what I noticed was that those descriptions didn't matter because my heart was already responding as intended. The more I learn, the more I realize that there are armies of artists and psychologists and directors combing through all of the complexities of music and weaving an experience for us. We get belted in for the Tilt-o-Whirl or Scrambler – and put ourselves in their hands.

I like to think of the Windsock man as an old friend. When he sees me coming, he can't stand the excitement – so he dances uncontrollably.

For us humans, our windsock nature begins very early. When babies get excited their arms and legs bounce uncontrollably. The energy – the feelings – find their way all the way out

through to their toes. Play peek-a-boo with them – and again – crazy arms and legs. Their bodies are doing the happy dance. No need to think about it – no learning necessary.

Our feelings are anchored in our bodies. We can watch someone walking down the street and have some indication of what they are feeling. We express ourselves – even unconsciously – through movement.

Have you ever noticed how some little boys carry themselves like their dads? And little girls don't? The cultures and groups we are in – or want to be in – let us know what it takes to belong. From the time we are born, we are surrounded by examples of proper gender, ethnicity, class, career, sexuality – perhaps even faith – comportment.

Although I wish I gave the impression of the fierce power and feminine strength of a flamenco dancer, I fear it's more like an Aunt Bea – small distracted dithering steps. My story gets told whether I want it to or not.

I also feel an affinity for the Michelin man – but let's not go there.

MUSIC AS CLIMATE CONTROL

Yes, we spend more when the music is right. Yes, we buy more French wine when Edith Piaf is singing. Indeed, we get a better sense of a company's brand. And, yes, the wait in line doesn't seem so long. Retailers have our number.

But the parallel truth is that we enjoy ourselves more. We feel better in a warm place – on both the Farenheit and emotional scales. The proprietors decide what they want our emotional state to be as we go about doing what we came in to do. And the amazing thing is – they almost always connect with a part of us. We may not be pop fans, but when we are looking to buy the perfect sweater? Bring it on.

This isn't limited to our shopping experiences. Dentists' and doctors' offices use it. Corporations and the DMV. Elevators. People are people wherever they go.

Emotional air freshener.

MUSIC CONNECTS US TO OUR PAST SELVES

I have read that the music from our teens and 20s will forever feel like our home base. It is forever entangled with our identity. The songs from our high school years don't just remind us of our struggles to belong, to be cool and accepted. Or of our first loves and first heartbreaks. Our first dances. Or the group experiences as we stood on the threshold of adulthood.

No, they don't just remind us. They take us there. We actually feel what we felt. For me? Well, when Elvis asks me if I'm lonesome tonight – and then he stops to just talk with me – I am right back there – swooning. Oh, Janis Joplin. Simon and Garfunkel – and, of course, The Beatles. Other people may appreciate their music. But, for me, it is woven into how I became who I am.

> *"If only the whole world could feel the power of harmony."*
> —Wolfgang Amadeus Mozart

Like a favorite hymn can shine light on our beliefs, this music shines a light on our dreams.

Music is a direct connection to our past selves. Some people who have experienced brain trauma or illness are only able to retrieve their memories – retrieve themselves – through music. Oliver Sachs discovered that people who have been long lost to dementia resurface when music from their early adult lives is replayed. For a few minutes they operate as they did then – humor, emotions, dancing. They even make flirty eyes.

"The past which is not recoverable in any other way is embedded, as if in amber, in the music, and people can regain a sense of identity. . . " — Oliver Sacks

Music is like the force of an electrical storm right in our hands. Given all this extraordinary power, I am thinking that, perhaps, music should be treated as a proper noun and always be capitalized. Anyone with me on that?

MAKE THE ORDINARY REVELATORY

It was the early 80's in Bath, Maine. It was a dark time for me. My mother and then my brother were fading from long battles with terminal illness. Weekdays were filled with work and worry. Evenings were spent giving care. But on the weekends, other family members stepped in giving me time to step away for a day or two.

My husband and I had a 23-foot I/O boat (for the uninitiated, that means a power boat) moored a few blocks away on the Kennebec River. Saturdays we would pack the kids and enough supplies for a day or a weekend, pull slowly away from the dock and head toward the ocean. After making the turn at the lighthouse, we'd navigate through the whirlpools and eddies of Hell's Gate.

> "Meanings of all songs come after they are recorded. Someone else has to interpret them." –John Lennon

Then the river widened out. It was at this point that we officially left the world behind. We would lean into the throttle – picking up speed until we were skimming – just flying - across the surface of the water.

Cue *The Miami Vice Theme Song* by Jan Hammer or Phil Collins' *In the Air Tonight*. It's hard to explain how that changed everything for me. Like I was riding away from the powerlessness of the rest of my life. I felt energy. Joy. Life was still surging on. I wish that sensation for everyone.

I'm sure you've all had those kinds of experiences. Sometimes a song will come on the car radio that catches something about the day or the scenery or the motion of the car – and the experience changes. This does come with risks. I have missed an exit or two when I am in that 'other' place.

Walking through the busy streets of New York City has always been inspirational. But – listen to a great choral piece – or anything by Morricone – and the beautiful becomes the sublime. All the ages and races. The Wall Streeters and the moms with kids. The heart-stopping moves of the bicycle messengers. For me, it's like a prayer.

Humans are the only species, as far as I know, that can be doing one thing and know that it represents another much bigger thing. We salute and it is more than a hand to the forehead. With music, life itself become palpable somehow. Present. We see things from a new perspective.

THE POWER AND JOY OF REWIND

Heraclitus said, "You cannot step into the same river twice." When we get lost in a song, it is a highly interactive experience. We feel. We react. Old memories are triggered. We imagine 'what if.' We touch spots in our psyche that need touching. Then we come home again, back to our 'real' lives. Aaaaand – play it again.

As Heraclitus wisely taught us, when we visit the song again – it is no longer the same song. It finds a new path – or a new us. It has more that it can give us – so we step back into that river.

It has always amazed me (well, frustrated is more accurate) that I never actually learn the lyrics to songs – especially the songs I love - while everyone around me can rattle off the words to every song they've ever heard –
seemingly without effort. Hey, when *Hamilton* became popular – there were kids singing more words per minute

> "When the music changes, the walls of the city shake." –Plato

than I had ever heard. And I was still struggling with the chorus. Apparently I was not in the room where it happened.

But I think I have figured it out. I am never really 'there' with the song – in its entirety. I leave – I go somewhere – immediately. I have favorite parts of songs that I keep missing – so I have to rewind in the middle of a rewind just to experience that moment (like moment 4:00 in Joshua Bell's *Rusalka*). I picture myself as a tetherball – orbiting wildly. But, hey. It's a great ride.

MUSIC IN OPEN CAR WINDOWS

Ahhh – warm weather. Ahhh – 5-second parties passing me by. As I sit waiting for grandkids to get out of school, I get glimpses into how these other drivers might be feeling at that specific moment. And suddenly I feel the same. We are actually connected.

It doesn't take but an instant for our bodies to inhale and react to any music. Once it goes through our ears, music has free-reign. Zap – I hear gospel and instantly feel inspiration, hope and kindness. Country? A little heartache – with a dose of resolve.

For that quick moment I am with them – the drivers. And perhaps that's one of the reasons why we all get such a lift when we drive open-windowed. It's a form of social radar.

DANCING AS A WEAPON OF WAR

Nothing seems to irritate power holders like having someone happily claim a space – and dance in it. Dancing with joy – and freedom – in the face of abuse gives the dancers power. Joy as a form of resistance. For example …

The Bomba, known as the dance of slaves in Puerto Rico, began on sugar plantations hundreds of years ago and is still celebrated today as part of the Black Lives Matter Movement. In the Holande section, the dancers mimic slave owners and their movements. How sweet that must feel!

> "Music occupies more areas of our brain than language does – humans are a musical species." –Oliver Sacks

The mocking theme was also beautifully carried out in the antebellum South. The Cakewalk, invented by African Americans, was intended to satirize the formal high society ballroom dances of plantation owners. Later, those same plantation owners came to think it was an effort to be like them. Ahhh – right under their noses – and hilarious, right?

Dance activism at Standing Rock in 2016 brought together hundreds of Ojibwe Jingle Dress dancers to support the water protectors below. Their dance, as with all Native American rituals, was once banned by the U.S. government. Like spirits rising from the past, their appearance on the crest brought hope and determination to the protestors.

Any time elders teach a new generation – any time brave souls perform for their fellow culture members - they take their lives in their hands. And they dance.

The U.S. has an especially brutal history in its efforts to eliminate the Native American culture. In 1890, several tribes whose populations had been decimated, who were barely surviving on barren reservations, danced their Ghost Dance to get back in touch with their 'Indianness'–

with their connection to community, history, families, and identity. They danced like their lives and their heritage depended on it. It was seen as such a national threat that the "Ghost Dance Wars" became the largest military campaign since the end of the civil war, involving a full third of the US Army. In the Wounded Knee Massacre, the 7th Cavalry killed over 250 Lakota, primarily unarmed women, children, and elders.

But the dance lives on. You can connect with the music and the dream with Robbie Robertson's *"Ghost Dance."* I have played it for my grandsons, usually getting emotional - struggling to tell them the story. If I had my way, it would be a required part of our holiday traditions — a retelling of the two cultures that came together to celebrate the first Thanksgiving. And how we lost our way for a while.

There are many other examples throughout history where indigenous dance has been banned, including the Hula, Tango, Flamenco, Irish Step Dancing, Chinese Shen Yun, Scottish Highland Dancing, Belly Dancing, the Sun Dance … You get the picture. In all cases the dances survive.

MUSIC TURNS BIG CONCEPTS
INTO SHARED EXPERIENCES

Admit it. The first few bars of *The Wedding March* get you a little choked up. We hear that song and together we appreciate the significance of the ceremony we are about to witness. Two lives are coming together. And, perhaps the biggest cultural concern - this partnership will bring the next generation into the fold. It is about survival as much as it is about love. When we hear those first few notes we experience our cultural values.

The *Pomp and Circumstance March* (and the ceremony surrounding it) helps the community process the importance of school graduation in our kids' lives. It is gut wrenchingly bittersweet because, as adults, we know — we really know — how much will change for them and for us.

These kinds of songs are cultural markers. They bring the culture's values into the room for all to share. They are community builders – social glue. Here are a few more.

Happy Birthday. Even strangers join in the song. The older we get, the more we recognize the fragility of life. And for the birthday star? How great is it that this celebration isn't about medals or accomplishments. It's the world saying it is happy they are here.

Patriotic songs conjure up the values of a nation. Anthems, for sure, do the job at events and celebrations but some popular songs pack a more powerful punch. Woodie Guthrie's, *This Land is Your Land*, Irving Berlin's *God Bless America* and *America the Beautiful* made so popular by Ray Charles, top the charts, bringing appreciation into people's every day lives. When we hear these songs, something stirs – but when we sing them in a crowd, we participate in the expression and commitment to those shared values. They mean something important in our lives.

And, of course, faith. Religions all around the globe – and across time – have used music to stir our souls. Choirs. Cantors. Call and response. Hymns sung by all. Organs that rattle our – well, they rattle our organs. It seems that everything, each part of the process, brings us deeper – and farther away from the outside world we left behind. Part meditation. Part prayer. Part contrition. Sung together.

BARCELONA

Barcelona street opera. In hindsight – no – in real time – it was one of those peak experiences. You know – the times when you are hyper-aware – watching and experiencing with every cell in your body. The experience of just bursting with – with - appreciation. I wish there was a bigger word. I was in Barcelona with my daughter and two of my grandchildren. We had just finished a lovely tapas meal in the old city – the part enclosed in a castle wall. As we wound our way

> "Sound is like a nutrient for your nervous system."
> –Prof. Dr. Alfred Tomatis

through the tall narrow passageways, I could hear a voice singing in the distance. After a couple of turns through the maze there he was at the end of an alcove – offering us his aria – his beautiful voice echoing and surrounding us and wrapping us in the theater and music of this perfect warm evening. Perfect acoustics. Perfect history. There were about a dozen other viewers scattered near us. When it came time for the chorus – half the people around me began to sing too with full operatic gusto. How amazing is this life! People living their culture as they had been doing for hundreds of years. And my eyes and ears – and heart - got to experience it with them. I don't think I have ever actually come back down to earth since then.

Culture and the arts aren't esoteric concepts. They are palpable forces in our every day lives. They lift and stretch us. Our bodies cease to constrain us.

So – music as entertainment? Sure. Music as protest? As testament? As social glue? As expression? As carrier of beliefs? As carriers of culture? As physical balm? As emotional balm? As climate control? As path to transcendence?

Can I get a 'HALLELUJAH?' (Cue the *Hallelujah Chorus*. Thank you, George Frideric Handel. We owe you one.)

BRINGING THE CONVERSATION ABOUT MUSIC TO CHILDREN

Music is a part of a child's life even before birth. Mom's constant heartbeat or the cadence of her walk feel normal. They hear the sounds - and the music - of her daily life. Once in mom and dad's arms, there are lullabies, tinkling mobiles, cooing. So much learning is enhanced with music. Has any child learned the ABC's without the accompanying song? Rhythm and clapping songs. Head & shoulders, knees and toes. Twinkle twinkle little star.

MUSIC MAKES OCCASIONS SPECIAL

When your family is on the way to a wedding, graduation, funeral, sports rally, etc. – make a habit of anticipating with your child what music they will likely hear. Help them begin to see the role music has in important life moments.

> *"We're off to a sports event. What music will be playing? What do they want people to feel? Can you think of some songs that definitely won't fit? Like "Lullaby and Good Night?" Have fun – get a little outrageous. Let's imagine if there was no music at all. How would that change things?" Share a wink when you both notice a song you predicted.*
>
> *"We're off to a religious service. What kind of music do you think we will hear? What role do you think music plays in the service? How would the service be different without music?" (Same process for weddings, funerals, holidays)*
>
> *"We're off to celebrate a graduation..."*

SOMETIMES MUSIC CAN HELP YOU FEEL WHAT YOU WANT TO FEEL

Work with one of your child's favorite songs from a movie. Explore the feelings the song may evoke (you may need to offer most of the possibilities). Just as an example, I am using *"Let it Go!"* From Frozen.

In the movie Elsa finds the courage to be herself, to be proud of who she really is. She knows that if she tells people more about herself, she might lose some friends. But she finds her courage and decides to do it.

"That's a feeling we all need to feel, isn't it? That's one of the reasons the song is popular. People want to feel that feeling over and over again. They want to connect with their courage." Tell them about a time that when you were growing up and found a helpful song. Sing it to them – and let yourself get emotional if that happens naturally. Their lives are just as tough as yours was.

It's a good thing if we want to listen to a song many times. It could be that our heart is telling us it needs some time to work on something. When you hear a song on the car radio that makes you feel something – talk about it. Ask if they get the same feelings. Make a habit of treating music as an invitation to talk about feelings.

LET'S GO ON A DANCING TRIP!

The purpose of this activity is simply to get your young children moving and dancing and enjoying themselves. They will feel proud when they can move into the next dance even before they see you doing it. And, obviously you will both feel the joy of doing the dances together.

The fun of this game is restarting and repeating each dance move before they discover the next one. Think "The 12 Days of Christmas" – for your feet (and the rest of your body too!) Make up your own stories and dances. The examples listed are meant to give you a sense of what a dancing trip can be. The sky's the limit with the fantastic worlds they can see on these journeys.

"We're going on an imaginary journey. (Start marching.) A special dancing journey. We travel by dancing. Join me." As you march, talk about some of the things you see. Point at them as if they are actually there. You see clouds, and oak trees aaaaaand pigs crossing the road doing BALLET! When you say ballet, do a fancy pirouette or plie for about 10 seconds.

Then begin again, marching, seeing clouds, oak trees and pigs doing ballet (that's the prompt to do ballet), then start pointing out other things you see – ie. a hot dog stand, a school bus with flashing lights aaaaand bears doing a hula dance. You all hula for about 10 seconds, then begin again - each time doing the dances mentioned.

Going on a marching trip ... ballet ... hula ... and now you see ...? Cows and kids on bikes and giraffes doing the twist. (Twist for a while, then begin again.) Marching, ballet, hula, twist and now you see .... dogs barking, a squirrel in a tree aaaaand – Grandpa tap dancing....

IN THE DIRECTOR'S CHAIR:
MOVIE & MUSIC DOUBLE FEATURE

One afternoon, watch a movie on television with your children. When it is over, watch it again with notebooks and notice when the music comes and goes.

What type is it? What do you think they wanted the music to do? Their attention will wane quickly - which is fine. You have now queued up the possibility of 'noticing' movie music at other times. Kudos to them when they become aware of music in a scene - and mention it to you.

MUSIC SLEUTH DISCOVERY WEEK

It is everywhere – almost invisible to us. For a week, everyone in the family makes a note each time they notice music. Keep a running list on the refrigerator..

Begin with a discussion about what counts as music. If your clothes dryer has 3 notes? Microwave? Do they count? Notice when you turn things on and off.

Be sure to notice when you are shopping, or each time you turn on your computer, or background to video games, or television shows, or elevators, or ..... ice cream trucks. You get the picture – or – the sound.

LYRICS HABIT: EXCUSE ME WHILE I KISS THIS GUY

The point is to engage with the music you and your child listen to. When you hear a song on the radio, if the lyrics are unclear, have some fun wondering what they might be? Get opinions. Bookmark websites so you can easily look up lyrics.

> *Did I just hear Annie Lenox sing, "Sweet Dreams are Made of Cheese?"*
>
> *Or Toto singing, "I bless the grains down in Africa.*

PUTTING DANCE INTO EVERYDAY ACTIVITIES

The lesson? Dancing can be fun, informal – and it feels good. Much of the learning will come from seeing you model in-the-moment fancy footwork. Standing at the stove stirring? Pick up a rhythm with your hips and feet and enhance it as you continue to stir. Show that it is natural to dance.

When you both have your feet on the floor, tap out a short rhythm. See if they can copy it with just a listen or two. Make it easy at first. They get to then tap out their own and you must try to repeat it.

> *When you are expecting a friend or family member to come to your front door, plan a full-family quick spin and welcoming bow as you open the door. Be fearless. You might give that person a heads-up so they can enter with a little flair too.*
>
> *Plan a tapping code. A secret rhythm that says "I love you." or "I'm getting bored." Only family members will know what it means.*
>
> *Begin a follow-the-leader routine as they follow you to the kitchen or the car. You do a step variation – and they follow. On your way back, they get to lead and you follow.*

SCHOOL DANCES

These conversation ideas can help your middle school child appreciate the social connection role of school dances. Being great at dancing is less important than enjoying your friends – to music.

School dances can be like Olympic events for our kids. They want desperately to belong. To not be ridiculed or marginalized. To show (some) competence. And to celebrate true friendships. They feel like all eyes are on them – because they are.

> *Explore the social and emotional aspects of school dances. Share stories and dances from when you were a teenager. Any favorite memories? Were you nervous?*
>
> *Q. What do you think makes a good school dance? How can you tell if people are having fun? Why do you think dances can make people feel nervous or uncomfortable? Can you show me how some of the kids in your class dance? Is there someone who dances like you would like to dance?*
>
> *If your child will accept help (not guaranteed), you can find very specific guidance online for many of today's 'moves.' Practice together (being careful not to learn too quickly.) Just mastering a few simple moves can take some of the edge off.*

CHAPTER 3

THEATER - WE ARE THE THESPIANS

It takes a lot of rehearsing for a man to be himself. - William Saroyan

First, some facts... I think my Art in Real Life quest began with acting. Of course I could act. Who didn't? Once I stepped outside my door I knew I was somehow on stage – that there were expectations of how I should act. By aligning how I spoke and moved I was able to connect. To belong. I behaved differently in church or school or with friends. With each scene change, I donned the appropriate role.

A few decades later I now understand how deeply embedded this impulse is to match those around us. Our mirror cells may actually be in the driver's seat more than we realize. Without thinking, we match posture, gestures and even gait. Aligning and connecting is so important to our species that it is an automatic impulse. We do it unconsciously. And it's not just the physical --- but the emotional story as well. We automatically wince when someone falls and we get a lump in our throats when we see someone in distress. We've all witnessed how quickly a baby's cry can spread to other babies in the room. We align. We connect.

Acting is not pretending. We act our age. We act like a manager – or a waiter – or a diva. We actively choose how we behave in our lives. These choices are honest expressions of the real us. I may be cranky on the inside, but when I am with a troubled friend, I put that aside because I know what the moment – and my friend – needs. I use the words I have learned. The tone of voice I have practiced. Becoming the adult version of ourselves takes years of observation, scripts, practice and feedback. Generations before us have learned what responses most simply and unambiguously keep and reinforce the connections. Each variation can open us up to being misunderstood. For many daily routines the mantra must be 'keep it simple.' Cleverness can confuse. The choreography of introductions, the rituals of grieving are all stylized – simplified - in the name of keeping us woven into a safe community. We don't have to start from scratch each time. We follow the scripts and all is well. "Thank you!" "You're welcome." "Gesundheit." "Have a nice day." "Keep the change." "How about dem Mets?"

"It's not easy being an actor, and having said that, everybody's an actor."
–Patti LuPone

If we want to run with our herd, we don't keep stopping the group with, "Can you slow down a minute? I'm not sure I want to go left." We go left. Yielding to "that's the way things are done" most of the time is one of the most human things we do. Ceremonies, rituals, holiday traditions, protocol - even etiquette - all showcase our values and keep us comfortably engaged with one another. Although there is always room for personal style, full abandonment of a group norm can bring our membership into question.

I'm reminded of the amazing flocks of starlings that move like a sensuous cloud at dusk. The living formation morphs and moves but, somehow, always stays together. These birds have found a way to benefit from the safety of the flock – discouraging predators – while responding to opportunities. That same impulse in humans may look a little different – but the survival strategy is the same.

LINE! CAN SOMEONE GIVE ME THE LINE!

You know what I mean. The trope of a stuffy old actor in rehearsal losing his place in the script, and he declares, "Line!" There have been sooooo many times in my life when I realized I didn't have the words I needed. If only I could just shout out, "Line!"

Our lives are filled with scripts - little snippets designed and supported by our culture. How great is it that we don't have to stop to think what to say with each new person we meet! Cultures are masterful at making social interactions easy because they know that integration and smooth operations help ensure the group's survival. Providing us with greeting menus (What's up!) and good-byes (See ya!) help us show one another that we are friend, not foe.

Obviously these vary around the globe and often we see regional differences too. Since my move to Philadelphia a few years ago, strangers greet me everyday with "Hon." Oh yes, a reminder that I am in a new environment.

As social beings, we thrive when we feel connected.

When I've waxed on enthusiastically about this idea that so many of our interactions are composed of cultural scripts, I often hear, "But, no, Susan. We need to be authentic." Authentic emphasized as if it is in opposition to using tried and true responses.

I grew up in a family that didn't socialize. Ever. Sometimes aunts, uncles or cousins would visit – but not often. So I wasn't exposed to the basic mechanics of greetings, introductions – initial small talk. Put me in a new situation where people were mingling and my standard – authentic – response would be to smile. Or smile and nod. I wanted people to know that I was happy. That I liked them. But I honestly didn't have the words they did. Line!!

My friend from Maine, Yvonne – the conversationalist – had just attended a play with me in NYC at a small theater on the East side. It took us a few blocks before we were finally able to catch a cab. We settled in and were chatting. At one point she had a comment about the play that I found interesting – so I was quietly giving it some thought when, out of the corner of my eye, I felt her staring at me. When I turned to her – she just kept staring. I asked, "What?" Yvonne, looking a bit confounded, said, "That's it?! You have nothing to say?" It took me a minute to realize that I had not yet responded to her last comment because – you know – I was thinking. So she taught me a lesson. "For God's sake, would it hurt you to just say something to let me know you

> "Sincerity is the most important thing in life.
> Once you can fake that,
> you've got it made."
> –George Burns

heard me?!" Uhhhhh. At this point I was racing to keep up. Exasperated, she said, "I hear ya! Next time try saying, 'I hear ya!'"

It isn't like I was raised by wolves but, for sure I had missed a few essentials along the way. At this point, an enthusiastic, "I hear ya!" from you all would feel just right.

Often children on the lower rungs of the social ladder lack these basic tools. Feeling (and acting) awkward in the most basic social situations can start to take its toll as soon as they start school. It continues to limit their options as they try to find work – and to find their own group of friends. Getting them comfortable with a fuller range of social scripts could help them move more freely in their world. Perhaps we could call it social health?

RELIGIOUS CEREMONIES

For me it was St. Patrick's Cathedral on Fifth Avenue. Or it could be any cathedral or temple or mosque. Places of worship – by design – by purpose – are built to bring people together – not just as observers but as participants. We humans have always needed to come together to share, to commit, to participate in stories that are about bigger things – much bigger things – than what our daily routines offer us.

I often visited St. Patrick's at the end of a workday or on a weekend stroll. The Gothic design makes being petty nearly impossible. The sounds are different. The light is different. The smells are different. Everything reminds us – no – takes us – to a higher plain. The soul-stirring, symbolic, metaphoric plain where we may use common words but we all know they mean something that words alone can't capture.

One day just before Easter, as I sat near the back of the church, a grand procession began from the right side of the altar. Bishop after bishop, priest after priest – all in full display of hierarchy. The line made it all the way to the back of the church and down the center aisle. And they kept coming. I would later learn it was the Chrism Mass – a celebration of the institution of the priesthood – and the annual blessing of all of the ceremonial oils used for the coming year.

With absolute respect – I say it was great theater. Every detail, every gesture, every reading, the music, the prayers, the costumes – planned and presented to ensure that everyone could experience the bigger story – the story about faith and commitment and reverence. There were no casual waves or stopping to chat. No. This was an ensemble piece recreating history. Parishioners were experiencing history.

So many of our religious ceremonies are – at their core – acting out important events and beliefs - together. And by acting them out together we communicate our membership to one another. There are words to be said. Very specific words.

And responses to be offered. Very specific responses. We bow our heads together. Or kneel – together. That's what membership looks like.

MOLLY – THE INSTRUCTOR WITH RED YARN HAIR

Those little cuties had no idea about the lessons they would really be learning that day. They thought it was about circles and all the things we can see in circles. As I sat at the head of the table going blah blah blah and handing out materials, a master class in student engagement was happening at the other end of the table. Her name was Molly and she was a hand puppet. Yes, an undercover instructor with red yarn hair. The children saw me treat Molly as I would any of them. Molly was just like any silly, fidgety, friendly child - with feelings.

I taught at the Blue School in New York City as it took it first steps into becoming a private independent school in Manhattan. The founding families were the three original Blue Men with their wives – and their adorable little kids - two of whom were my very own grandbabies. The core commitment was to develop a new approach to education – one that maintained kids' sense of wonder and curiosity. One where they would learn kindness and belonging. I was there as part of the launch team before going back to work in the corporate world.

The first class was made up of nine toddlers, ranging in age from two to four years old. For most, this would be their first 'structured' learning – other than a few Mommy & Me music classes offered in the neighborhood. We knew these first few months could lock in their expectations about education for a long time - and we wanted those expectations to be high.

I worked with Sam, a puppeteer who was relaxed and playful – happiest when she was working with kids. Her role – Molly's role – was to blurt out questions she thought might be on the other kids' minds and to engage directly with them. Molly would lean over to Iris and say, "Iris – I like that line you did. Can you show me how to do that?" "Oh, Leah, wow – look at what you did." "Susan, can you come help me?"

Sometimes Molly was silly; she would just start laughing a silly laugh.

By the end of that first 'lesson,' those little cuties were no longer staring up at me with big scared eyes. No. They had relaxed – at least a little. They were getting to know their classmates – at least a little. They all felt they had a new friend. Her name was Molly.

Here's the thing. Have you ever noticed how quickly and naturally kids relate to puppets? Talk about unbiased! It doesn't matter if the puppet is green or fluffy – or a stick with two googly eyes, If that puppet turns to them, they respond. And they don't get tense or nervous. They simply listen – and relate.

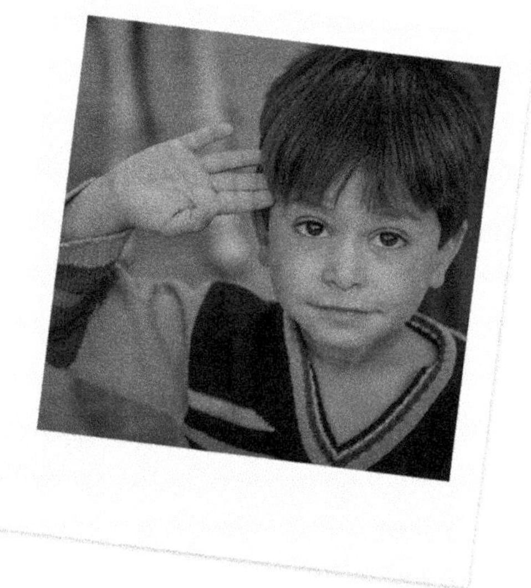

It's akin to magic. When children console a scared puppet, they aren't pretending. They are actually consoling the puppet. When a puppet engages them in silly talk, the kids aren't pretending to be in a conversation – the ARE in a conversation. The time I used puppets at an HR meeting while at L.L.Bean – well – let's just say that didn't go so well. Grown-ups! They can be so stuffy

THE THEATER OF PROTESTS

The public square has always been a place where ideas and stories are marketed along with the requirements of everyday life. Take a soapbox, find a space – and draw people in. Governments, religious organizations and brotherhoods have held public ceremonies and spectacles for all to see - public displays of their values and their influence. Our history in the US includes swearing in ceremonies, ticker tape parades and, horrifyingly, public lynchings. All meant to send messages about power.

I was in college in the late sixties. You know the time. Vietnam war. Gloria Steinam v Phyllis Schlafly. The draft. Hippies. "All we are saying – is give peace a chance." Many people, college age particularly, wanted change. And I was one of them. We knew that changing a system wouldn't happen easily – if at all. So week after week, month after month, we gathered and planned. How do we get the message out there? How do we tell the stories so they will be noticed - and felt? Symbolism – daisies in guns, peace symbols and peace signs. Songs of protest. Sit-ins. And marches that filled the streets. Planned. Choreographed. Scripted. Amplified. Bullhorns were everywhere and they invited everyone into the show. Into the performance.

We were acting out our resistance.

BRINGING CHARACTERS INTO THE ROOM

We've all done it. We're in the middle of a conversation and, in the process of retelling a story we not only quote someone – but we step into their character as they would have said it. Admittedly, some of us are better at that than others – but we do it automatically. We know that words alone don't tell the whole story. It's that snippiness we want to capture – or that heat – or that innuendo. And who, really, can say Stella – calmly. We become Marlon Brando for an instant.

Each of us carries our history, our preferences, our learning in different ways. Our gender, class and ethnicity play a role in how we present ourselves. Our pace. Our posture. Our comfort with eye contact. So when we want to bring someone into the conversation vicariously – it begins with an unconscious shape-shifting to capture the full picture.

A bunch of us were chilling in the dorm lounge - talking about a grumpy history professor.

I just naturally stood up and walked – in his character - as I was retelling a story. Of course I did – I thought everyone did. But it was another one of those wonderful college experiences where you suddenly discover that what you see as normal – well – may not be so common. Everyone started to laugh – hard. "How do you do that?" "OMG – you've captured him." Soon I was taking requests. "Walk like …" I became a lounge act – a college dorm lounge act. But since that day I have learned to limit my performances to family and close friends. I share my 'gift' more carefully.

Okay, right now, imagine that were sharing a story about the Dalai Lama. Bring him into the room for us.

NOMINEE FOR MOST APPRECIATED SCRIPT
GOES TO: LITTLE WHITE LIES

Where would we all be if we felt permission – or even obliged – to publish every thought we have! Civilizations (root word 'civil') have thrived because we are raised to recognize the value of protocol and principles that keep kindness on the forefront.

We all live our imperfect lives – clothes that don't fit perfectly, hair that isn't cooperating. We use the wrong word - or worse – the wrong name. We know it and feel it and carry it and still muster up the courage to come back another day. To try again. We've all been there so we follow The Golden Rule. When we notice someone having an 'off' experience, we lie. I mean, we do unto others …

When someone says to me with believable enthusiasm, "Hey, you look great," I assume they mean – it looks like you tried – and that's good enough. To that I say thank you.

PERSONA – OUR MASK

If I asked you all to – right now – take off your mask for a while, you would know exactly what I meant. It's that face we present to the world every day – or most days. It's our deal with the culture to play by group rules enough to maintain stability – and keep us all safe. A group without basic cohesion is a group at risk. So we do our part to contribute. Most of us can take that mask off at times.

Where did we get that mask? Who decided?

By the time our children go to school – by
they time they make their first appearance in the
outside world – they pretty much understand the
role they will be playing – the mask they will wear.
Families and cultures make sure they do. We are all
born into a place and time – with certain physical
characteristics – surrounded by a constellation
of main characters in our lives. We can't choose
to be in another play. "Wait! Wait! I'd rather be
born white, male in an affluent family blessed
with exceptional talent, amazing good looks and
physical strength!" Nope. By the time we would be able to say that – we
have been tattooed. (But that's another chapter.)

MASKS

Masks can be sticky. Sometimes we forget we are wearing one and proceed – inappropriately.
When I was at L.L.Bean, heading up organizational learning, I spent my days developing ways to
engage employees – ways to create an
environment where learning happened
organically. I loved it. I spent evenings
reading the latest management trends.
Stacks of Harvard Business Reviews
everywhere. Many of my work friends
had become personal friends – family
friends.

"Young people, who are still uncertain of
their identity, often try on a succession of
masks in the hope of finding the one which
suits them –the one, in fact, which is not a
mask."
–W. H. Auden

In my sad case, one evening I actually set up a flip chart in my home when it was time to
discuss vacation options. Yep – I'm not proud – but I share it because it is a perfect example of
a sticky mask. But you needn't worry. The kids spotted it right away. My twelve-year-old said,
"Mom. This is not L.L.Bean." Point taken.

Nope – got nothin.'

Oh wait! Other than CHARADES! Come on people! We all become Marcel Marceau in our living rooms. Some of us get stuck behind those invisible walls. Or – wait - when someone is on the phone and we want to give them a message like "I'm leaving now – to walk the dog." Or the "I'm hanging myself out of boredom" gesture. There's always the proverbial, "I'm pretending not to hear you by poring over this newspaper – or cereal box" bit.

We all have an inner Marcel Marceau. The 'call me later' gesture is the cost of entry into his realm.

21 STEPS – 21 SECONDS – 21 STEPS

The choreography of reverence and honor. Cultures and communities have long used the arts to help members focus – and FEEL – together. Celebrating births, graduations and weddings. Giving awards for success and efforts. Religious traditions bring us together to strive to be better people – and better souls.

But the idea that a community or nation can ask members to give their lives for the greater good – well – that is a very big ask. And yet, the world over, we see that kind of sacrifice. Cultures raise their children to see the heroic nature of joining the military or law enforcement or … the list goes on.

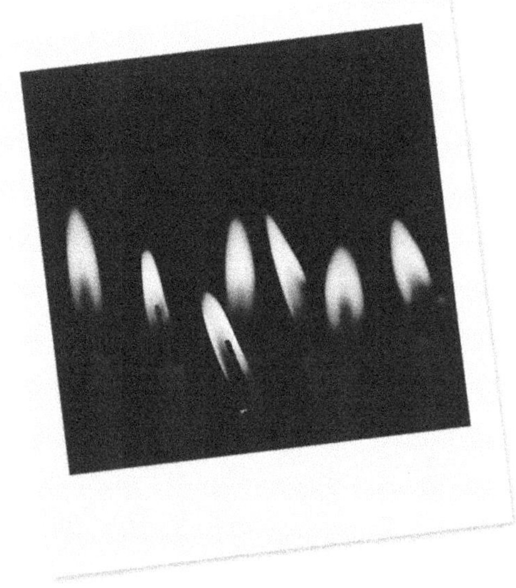

At the Tomb of the Unknown Soldier at Arlington National Cemetery, we see the pinnacle of performance. Absolutely every detail is controlled because the sentinels and the observers are in a very sacred space and moment – trying to express boundless gratitude for the ultimate gift. Participation at the ceremony is a privilege and any sign of disrespect prompts immediate attention.

Today, all Sentinels are volunteers. They are all between 5-foot-10 and 6-foot-four, with a proportionate weight and build. They know the grave locations of nearly 300 veterans, and they are able to recite seven pages of Arlington Cemetery history word for word. They walk at a pace of 72 beats per minute, and they spend hours practicing their steps with a metronome. They get haircuts twice a week.

For 24 hours a day, 365 days a year, guards whose uniforms show no sign of rank, take 21 steps, pause for exactly 21 seconds and return the 21 steps. After another 21-second pause the process begins again. Every detail – the precise choreography, the impeccable uniforms, the stylized rituals – are all designed to help us feel what we need to feel.

Sacred theater. Blessed are the keepers of this ceremony.

THEATER – IN REAL LIFE

For about ten years I lived in a small apartment on the third floor at Astor Place in New York City - just above The Blue Man marquee. It was in The Colonnade building, built in the 1830's and it faced the Public Theater across the street. The Public Theater was commissioned by the Astor family in the 1850's to house the first great library accessible to the public. Looking out my windows, all I could see was history. And if I looked down, all I could see were the arts – and lines of patrons. If heaven had a zip code, it would be right there.

> "Pretending to be other characters helps teach the important moral development skill of empathy." –scholastic.com

The Public Theater breathed performances and audiences in and out seven days a week. Often performers at Joe's Pub, after finishing their live shows, would have a phalanx of happy customers follow them out to the sidewalk. Still on a high, they would pull their instruments back out and continue the performance.

I detected these gatherings within seconds. I would run down the stairs, out the door and across the street to be a part of the audience. To breathe in the moment.

Most of these impromptu events happened in the evening. But one special day, the cast preparing for a reboot of *Hair* assembled on the sidewalk and did a few exciting absolutely perfect numbers. Perfect multipart harmony. I could hardly contain myself. The group broke up and dispersed, with four of five of them crossing the street so, of course, I followed them. Within a minute there was another short vignette – a short play – happening right in front of me.

I was in heaven seeing these pros take us into a story so quickly. After a couple minutes the group dispersed again – some heading back across the street toward the corner bus stop. Of course I followed – eager to get another 'front row seat.' This time there was a young couple, about a foot in front of me, having a conversation. I stood there, almost breathing the same air, excited to see what they would do. The bus came. They boarded and away they went. I looked around at the other 'audience' members and suddenly realized that this wasn't a theatrical performance.

Uhhhhh. Well THAT was awkward.

Art. Real life. Sometimes it's hard to tell the difference.

QUIET DOWN

One of my early roles at L.L.Bean was working the Customer Service desk. I absolutely loved it – made great friends – took pride in being able to snap through a stack of bills with accuracy and efficiency – ship items around the world – replace parts of treasured old ski sets. My customer count was good. Mystery shoppers gave me great ratings. I was riding high – until, that is, I got my performance review.

> "Women speak two languages – one of which is verbal."
> –William Shakespeare

My supervisor, after reviewing all my numbers, told me that, despite those metrics, she wouldn't be giving me a 5. Blink. Blink-blink. What?

"Susan, you have an unprofessional laugh. I am giving you a 4 rating. "If you want to fit the role, your laugh needs to change." Blink. Blink-blink.

I had heard my laugh described as hearty before – or infectious – but never unprofessional. But I 'got it.' I understood what she was saying. It could be a distraction. She was saying I didn't fit the part – yet.

Within a week I had modulated it down a few notches. I thought about just not laughing – and instead saying "Hey. That's funny." Social bonding would have been out the window with that option. So I found a middle path. A little less Meg Ryan and a little more Mother Theresa. Until, that is, I punched out and headed home.

BRINGING THE CONVERSATION ABOUT
THEATER & RITUALS TO CHILDREN

Children are master pretenders. They don't just play a part. They play all the parts. They work through their issues over and over. One day you'll see play figures crying for mommy. Another you will overhear one being mean to the others. And of course there are the uncomfortable times when you see lots of figures missing limbs – or their heads! It's a scary world and there is much readying to do.

Practice makes perfect. Theater skills are central to our children's (and our own) development, helping them understand and manage how they express themselves with their bodies, voices and words. Self-expression in context. Social skills. After all, we all know that "all the world is a stage," right?

ACTING: INSIDE - OUTSIDE

This discussion can help your child appreciate that there is a difference between having feelings and showing feelings. It gets right to the heart of children's constant struggle between belonging and being special.

> *"Notice people walking down the street. What do you think that person might be feeling? What clues are you using?" Get them to notice, not just facial expressions, but body language. If someone feels happy, show me how they might show they are happy. Sad. Tired. Frustrated. Scared. Lonely. Join in.*
>
> *Then – try combinations. If someone was happy and tired .....? Angry but in a hurry? Take turns making up combinations the other has to do. Get silly.*
>
> *"Can you think of times when someone might choose to act happy even if they weren't happy?" Share some personal stories from when you were a child when you didn't want others to know what you were really feeling. An obvious example is the pressure kids feel NOT to cry.*
>
> *"Can you think of times when it is important NOT to hide your real feelings?" Share a few examples of times when you took a stand and told someone what you really felt in the moment even though it was difficult to do.*

LIFE SCRIPTS

Children need to learn how to interact in basic social situations politely and with confidence. Basic greetings, introductions, Thank You's, table skills, holding doors, etc. Children who have these skills under their belts will be able to find their way in the world more comfortably and successfully.

Children can understand that manners help people feel at ease and safe. On your way to a social event, make a habit of reviewing the basics. Practice - have a little fun. "You did better this time. Soon you'll be a pro." "I like that you really tried today. That was wonderful.".

PUPPETS!!!!

Puppets can stimulate children's imagination, encourage creative play and discovery. But the most glorious power of puppets is that, when your child engages with them, their reaction is real. If the puppet is sad, your child will automatically try to comfort – not pretend to comfort. If the puppet keeps interrupting them, your child will deal with the problem – not pretend to deal with the problem. By bringing stuffed animals or other inanimate objects to life, you have the opportunity to deal with real feelings or events in their lives.

Consider having a puppet who always seems worried about growing up. They can turn to you or your child for assurance. The puppet can do something a little rude, then deny doing it. Help your child encourage the puppet, to show that they understand how hard it can be sometimes to admit doing something wrong.

One of the special powers of theater is that, by bringing a character to life, the actor is able to relate to that character's real experience. It can bring insights, empathy and self awareness. The purpose of these activities is to help your child step into new worlds easily and playfully. When you meet them in that pretend world, all sorts of new discoveries await. This exercise can help your child step into pretend easily, unselfconsciously.

Let's pretend to be ... animals. See if you can guess what animal. Then – pretend to be a cow who wants all the daisies but the other cows are eating them too quickly. A butterfly who can't decide what pretty flower to visit. A dog who can't remember where he buried his bone.

Then – move on to people and situations. First, pretend to be a fussy baby. (Kids LOVE to be fussy babies.) Someone who is too tired to eat their meal. Someone who doesn't want to wake up. A barber with dull scissors. A grandmother learning to jump rope.

You can make a routine of anticipating upcoming, perhaps stressful, situations. Play out ways they could deal with them. Let's pretend all the kids at the party are talking and someone feels left out. What might we say or do to help?

SENIOR THESPIAN – YOU!

Become a haughty queen as you serve lunch. Insist on silly rituals in order to be allowed to eat. A king who doesn't recognize most of his utensils. A cowboy who reads nighttime stories. A French painter who is fussy about setting the table. A newscaster reporting on what the child is doing. An astronaut floating around. Someone who just doesn't want to be seen.

DIFFERENT SCENE. DIFFERENT PERFORMANCE.

The purpose of these discussion ideas is to help children recognize that we all adjust how we act based on context – and that can be a good thing. An easy way to introduce this concept can be as you prepare to attend an event with a little more formality than what they are accustomed to.

"We're going to Auntie's wedding and its important that we all are ready to help make it special. Not only do we dress up a little, we also want to be sure we don't distract from their celebration. So we will be sure to sit still during the ceremony.

And we will practice good manners by introducing ourselves to new people ..."

Can you think of other situations where people act differently?

RELIGIOUS RITUALS AS THEATER

Explain that all religions perform rituals to explain and remember the stories and values important to their faith. Acting out ceremonies and rituals gives us all a chance to participate - together. It's a way we show membership - that we believe the same things.

CHAPTER 4

STORYTELLING

"How did we get here? How can I stay safe? Why was that person mean to me?"
Have a seat, my friend, and I will tell you a story. It will explain everything.

Humans are blessed with an evolutionary advantage; we can transmit deep concepts and complex information to one another. Lessons learned over generations are passed down. How to hunt. When to plant. How to protect ourselves from those people on the other side of the mountain. Where to buy the best cappuccino.

Origin stories. Exquisite myths. Tales from travelers. Wonderings about the stars above and the seasonal winds. Lessons about the consequences of personal ambition or jealousy or vanity. All told and retold because, from the beginning, humans were curious about the big questions. And we were especially curious about one another – about human nature.

We discovered that giving guidance like, "Be prepared!" or "Be kind," got a yawn from listeners. But – put those lessons in a story about King Midas or Chicken Little – and ta-da – people happily gave their gold away. Well – maybe not happily.

Stories were memorized and shared across generations. Then – drum roll - reading and writing came onto the scene! Talk about a huge – and recent - evolutionary jump!

Spoken language has been around for 600,000 years. We have had clothing for over 150,000 years. We have danced – forever. We have been using images and symbols for over 100,000 years. Reading and writing? A mere 6000 years. And it was a doozy of a leap – requiring nearly every part of our brain to work concurrently.

"Those who tell the stories rule society." —Plato

5,400 years ago writing was invented in Southern Mesopotamia, present-day Iraq. Around 23 B.C., books simultaneously appeared in Rome, the Middle East and several Asian nations. Good news traveled quickly. And, the piece de resistance, in 1450 Johannes Gutenberg perfected the first commercial printing press. The world – and the human race - would never be the same.

Books launched the Renaissance. Martin Luther's writings changed people's relationship with their faith and their god. The scientific revolution was enabled when scientific findings were published. Revolutionary ideas could bring the masses together to challenge power sources. Would the American Revolution have succeeded without Thomas Paine's *Common Sense* stirring up colonists' outrage?

Reading is no simple thing. Just think of the complexity. Once our eyes see the symbols, we have to interpret those little lines into letters, then the letters into sounds – combining them with other letters to form words, and determining what those words mean, in that sentence, spoken by that character. At the same time our emotional systems are charged as we empathize with the character. We feel real fear or real exuberance. Our memories come rushing in. When we read 'grasp', the parts of our brain supporting our hands light up. The parts of our brain that help us speak are engaged, even if we are reading silently. All these areas are operating together and integrating with the speed of light because here comes another word and another meaning and feeling and ....

The real hero of this story is our brain's white matter. White matter is the Slip 'n Slide of our brain – the busiest fastest communication highway we could imagine. All those flashes find their way to all of the other centers so an integrated understanding and experience can happen. Instantaneously. And continuously.

When we are reading, our brain is all in. It doesn't care if our body is strapped in a middle seat on a flight to Denver. While we are in the book, our brain is really in the book. We are in a boat – with a Tiger. Or we are with Jay Gatsby when he sees Daisy looking his way. Those little hashes and lines on a page have worked their magic. When we close the book, the memories of those experiences mingle with our 'real life' experiences. They become one more element in our bag of wisdom - fueling understanding and empathy. The more we read – the more we grow. And, back to the science of it all, the more we read the more our white matter grows. All book subtitles could be, White Matter Galore.

Storytelling has a big story to tell. It is everywhere in our lives. We expect and consume stories so naturally that we often fail to notice the impact they have on us. And we also fail to see ourselves as weavers of stories. Like the time I ......

WINNIE THE WHO?

The stories from my early childhood were ... let's say ... unconventional. Although Mom occasionally read a chapter or two from Uncle Wiggley, most of the stories I remember came from an old radio on a table beside my bed. Mom would turn the dial through squeaking channels until she got to Fibber McGee and Molly, Amos and Andy, Our Miss Brooks or Edgar Bergen's ventriloquist show (where I got to know the puppets Charlie McCarthy and Mortimer Snerd. Just think about that for a minute – I listened to a ventriloquist – on the radio.) Whatever was on each night – those were the characters that kept me company as I drifted off to sleep.

No *Winnie the Pooh* for me. Or *Charlotte's Web*. Instead of the Hundred Acre Wood or a charming old barn filled with lessons about life – I was picking up the rhythms of early sitcoms.

The one-line retorts. The 'charming' side of silly or lazy or fussy characters – but characters who were all, nonetheless, redeemable. To this day, I swear my brain has a joke ready to roll at any given moment. Badum-pssh! Thankfully I have learned to temper it – somewhat. It is an impulse that is not always good. Life is not always funny.

Although they wouldn't ever qualify as artistic narrative, these radio shows all had an arc to them. Glimpses into relationships, a little disappointment – perhaps some teasing – then redemption – easy redemption. A little brouhaha – then back to normal. That's what life is like, right?

Except it isn't always. My family – well – we stumbled over long-held grudges all the time. They hung in the air. No happy hugs – just another day – and another day. But those silly stories? Listening to them alone – at night? The absolutely dependable happy endings? I believed that they were real life - except perhaps the applause part. "Once upon a time … and they lived happily ever after."

I came to believe that humor could be a healing ingredient. Not many kids would list Lucille Ball as their hero, but, hey – their loss, right? Badum-pssh!

Later, when it came time for me to read the classics to my babies, I would often get a bit verklempt at how touching the stories and characters were. I met Winnie the Pooh when I was in my twenties. Awwwwww – he was just sweet and kind. No laugh track. No put-downs. Who knew!

WANT TO MAKE A DIFFERENCE?
TELL A COMPELLING STORY

I taught school for one year. One long year. It turns out it was the art I liked in art education – not so much the education part. But I will forever remember the privilege I had while I was there heading up a citywide Disability Awareness Week. Our goal was to get the town – not just the students – to appreciate, include and support citizens dealing with any kind of disability.

(Time reminder: An early target was to eliminate the term 'crippled' from people's vocabulary – which, unfortunately, was commonly used. I appreciate that the language is being updated again.)

After a few months of planning with other teachers and students, we launched our storytelling initiative. For one week, we would bathe people in Bath with story after story about real people. Neighbors. Friends. Blind people visited classrooms and workplaces to sit and chat about how they kept track of their wardrobes and folded their bills so they wouldn't inadvertently tip with a twenty-dollar bill. People in wheelchairs chatted about what they found difficult and what they did for fun. There was humor and warmth and idiosyncrasies everywhere. Each day we had students visiting stores in wheelchairs, or wearing blindfolds –'walking a mile in their shoes' - and later telling their stories to fellow students and their parents.

When the week was over, and with the encouragement of all the 'student-citizens,' we started seeing changes throughout the community. Even the Post Office put in a new ramp with a more gradual incline. People could understand immediately the impact of the changes they made. This wasn't about fundraising. It was about encouraging changes in all of our lives.

We were lucky. We happened on an approach that worked. We used it because it was affordable and scalable. Now we understand more about the reasons it was successful.

A few years ago, Pulitzer Prize-winning journalist, Nicholas Kristof, wrote about research into what makes people give to charities.

"This research arose when I was writing about Darfur for my column for The New York Times back in 2004. I was going to villages that had been burned out, talking to people who were survivors of massacres and it was frustrating me that I couldn't get people to pay more attention to this. Meanwhile, at that very same time here in New York City, there was a red tailed hawk called Pale Male that had been kicked out of its nest in Central Park and New York was all up in arms about this homeless hawk. And I thought, how is it that I can't generate as much passion about hundreds of thousands of people being slaughtered as people feel for this hawk."

> "Civilization began the first time an angry person cast a word instead of a rock."
> – Sigmund Freud

Why do we do that? I too was enthralled – a little outraged – about Pale Male. I too read the story every day – worried about what we were doing in general to our earth and fellow creatures. I immediately read any new news about him. Each day brought the next part of the story.

At the same time I knew all about Darfur – and famines. There were endless images of the unbelievable scale of the tragedy. There were numbers. And maps. And projections. But it seemed like each day was the same. Yep, still horrifying. Yep, still tragic. Of course I donated – once. But then …. How does one incorporate those truths into our minds and still just go about our day? Somehow we do. Detachment as a survival technique?

Research tells us that we all want to connect with other individuals. Not causes. And definitely not data. If we can see that our involvement actually has an impact on one person's life, we continue to invest effort or money. When a charity invites us to make a difference in the life of a child with a name and a story – we feel more compelled to give. But – and this is amazing - if we add a second child to the invitation, another child with a name and a story, contributions drop significantly. If we give dry statistics, donations drop like a rock.

Stories touch us – they reach us. We see the arc. It reminds me how, even though there are thousands of data points about George Washington, nearly every child in America remembers, "I cannot tell a lie. I chopped down the cherry tree." Man, that's a story we can all relate to, right? That's getting to know a hero.

YOU'RE SUCH AN EAGER BEAVER!

Metaphor mania. Okay, metaphors, similes – heck – delicious wordplay. Our brains love the leaps from thorny bushes to prickly relatives. From a slippery hillside to a slippery co-worker. It's about noticing patterns from our physical world – from our endlessly complex physical world – and picking up on those same patterns in our social world. Ahhhh, patterns. When we read – or hear – those words, our brains can conjure up all the physical attributes in an instant and superimpose them on a different subject. People from the rural Midwest might use terms like "corny" or "soft as a horse's nose" while those of us from New England might refer to "drawing a line in the sand" or 'The waves licked my toes."

When I was a young mom, I read everything I could get my hands on that might help me be the parent I wanted to be. I felt free to find a new way. A liberated way – unhooked from what I had experienced – and from the kind of conventional wisdom that might recreate the past. I tapped into philosophy, anthropology, medical advice, memoirs and poetry. But there was one book that simply came from a different place – that somehow packed all of my liberal hippie POVs and language into a new insight - The *Metaphoric Mind*, by Bob Sample. In it he explores why people raised in more rural natural settings are better able to tap into the richness of metaphoric thinking. Those living in inner cities simply have less exposure to nature's complexities – and therefore less access to patterns that can teach. I was so happy to be able to send my kids out into the field in all seasons. They knew the weight of dew. The crispiness of first frosts. The smell of freshly turned sods. Bramble. The color and smell of moss on trees. Like a balanced diet for their brains.

> "The purpose of a story is to be an axe that breaks up the ice within us." – Franz Kafka

Brain imaging studies have shown that when we read, "she had a rough day' the tactile regions of our brain are activated. "He's so sweet" wakes up our taste centers. Metaphor and simile rich text can be like a full brain workout.

Years later, while I was working in New York City, I was with a young mom whose 2-year old son cried when he first put his bare feet onto the grass in Central Park. I wished for those little toes to have some real grass time. (Of course there may be reasons to be careful about where to put your feet in Central Park.)

Researchers have found that, on average, people use a metaphor every twenty words. I have listed just a few below – focusing just on terms we use to describe people. You may find a simile or two. Linger just a sec over each, appreciating how they capture complex patterns in just a word or two. See if each phrase conjures up someone you know.

Enjoy.

Early bird. Lame duck. Sitting duck. Night owl. Love birds. Spring chicken. Looney. Chick. Peacock. Cock of the walk. Crusty. Batty. Fly by night. Flighty. Henpecked. Shark. Barracuda. Fish out of water. Crabby. Swimming upstream. Swimming against the tide. Lemmings. Cool as a cucumber. Corny. Apple of my eye. Peach. String bean. Salty. Sour grapes. Hotdogger. Saucy. Cheesy. Wet noodle. Thorny. Shrinking violet. Rosey. Wallflower. Coyote. Badger. Paper tiger. Bull in a china shop. Long in the tooth. Foxy. Horse's (butt). Weasel. Mousey. Stallion. Filly. Snake. Louse. Horse of a different color. Chameleon. Busy bee. Bees knees. Pack rat. Green with envy. Red hot. Yellow. Blue. Tough as nails. High strung. Built. Train wreck. Stacked. About to explode. Broken record. Bleeding heart. Spacey. Cute as a button. Spitfire. Old school. Fit to be tied. Loose cannon. Off their rocker. Pistol. Brown nose. Hard nosed. Sharp as a tack. Diamond in the rough. Granola. Helicopter mom. aaaaand ... (it's your turn.)

GOSSIP - VALUES POLICE

Shhhh. Lean in. I have something to tell you. Did you hear about ....? But you can't tell ANYONE!

Hooked! Try to look away! What is a culture to do! It defines its core values – deciding what is most important in members' lives. It might publish a list of 'rules to be followed – behaviors that are acceptable." And there is always a longer list of unmentionable or more sensitive rules. Cultures feed kids and adults a steady diet of stories about heroes who model the values – and consequences for those who don't. It gives awards and celebrates models of good behavior. And still – people stray!!!!

So cultures figured out a way to put enforcers right at our kitchen tables. In our congregations. Our workplaces. On periodicals vying for our attention in the grocery check-out lines. In social media. Everywhere. We can't escape.

> "A lie travels round the world while truth is putting her boots on." – Edgar Allan Poe

"Did you see the dress that girl was wearing? If she was MY daughter ...." "I heard that the Jones' had to pay off a teacher to get their son a passing grade?"

Just think of the power those storytellers have. Anytime I hear gossip I am reminded of how eager people are to show belonging – to show that they are 'good citizens' by pointing out the violators. Not admirable, perhaps – but understandable. "Did you see how much weight Susie put on? She better be careful. Her husband already has eyes out for the ladies." "Have you noticed Timmy still hasn't dated a girl?"

It's not all bad. I do believe that some gossip is truly about looking out for one another. Keeping order in a good way. I also think that this kind of enforcement role is one that women, primarily, have adopted. Perhaps it has been a way to balance the business, political and family power men have long enjoyed. It might be an even match.

As a child, much of what I learned about life — about what is acceptable — about how the world really works — came from overhearing adult conversations. I came to see that the gossip network was faster than any electrical circuits. And it carried the same amount of voltage — the ability to stun and burn.

THE IMPORTANCE OF
LIFE SCRIPTS IN EDUCATION

"I'm sorry." Just two words that make some of us start to sweat.

But without being able to express regret, we lose touch with those we love. We can't wipe our slates clean and just find new family or friends. It's inevitable that, within minutes, we will mess up again. The only way to clean things up — to stay connected with one another — is to apologize.

We first learn how to greet and how to say good-by - how to thank - to invite - to console - to ask for forgiveness - in our homes. For most kids, they begin school at least familiar with - comfortable with - these pivotal conversations. For most, this system works beautifully. But for some ...

Kids growing up in imperfect homes may not even be aware of the need to apologize - or welcome - or thank. They don't know how it sounds - how it looks - how it feels. These gaps can (will) get them marginalized at the starting gate.

Can we imagine a world where kids can not only learn about gravity and long division and conjugating verbs - but a world that will also get them ready to belong - to be trusted and accepted?

I had worked with Patrick when he was President and COO at Blue Man Group. A few years later we bumped into one another in a lunch line at Pret a Manger, a few months after he became the Executive Director at The Public Theater. Patrick was always a friend – kind and steady - in whatever he did. I was happy when he invited me to meet with him to explore his new world with an organizational culture lens.

The Public Theater was thriving. Oskar, the beloved Artistic Director, was an inspirational and ambitious leader, respected by artists and employees alike. Put a bunch of creative risk takers (senior staff and artists) in a room – and you better stand back when the door opens. Possibilities. So many possibilities. "We can find a way if …" And they kept finding ways. For a while.

The Public had begun running multiple shows concurrently – some uptown and some downtown. Very big award-winning shows along with smaller works by new playwrights. They had also expanded the types of programming beyond main stage, Shakespeare in the Park and

Joe's Pub to include Under the Radar, Public Works, and a Mobile Unit - each with a different purpose and audience. The staff was masterful at producing great theater. What they hadn't yet learned was how to manage the complexity that comes with sharing space, resources, technicians and other staff. Everything was a priority. It really was. Reputations were on the line. No employee wanted to be responsible for dropping the ball – but now there were balls being tossed from every direction. They were feeling at risk. When conflicts arose, "Let's ask Oskar" or "Let's ask Patrick" were the answers of choice. Straight to the top. Strong charismatic leaders can be wonderful – but they can, inadvertently, render all the levels below them impotent. No one wants to bother with those in-betweeners. Going to the top was evidence of status. It was a form of payoff for all the hard work.

The Public Theater had always been a gathering organization. Employees relished full company meetings where Oskar, Patrick and the CFO would take the stage and tell the Public Theater story. "Here's who we are. Here's what we have accomplished. Here's what we want to do." People felt they could ask or say anything and that they would be told the truth. Every staff meeting was basically the same – hear from the top.

In organizational development vernacular – company heroes are those who get airtime. Whatever values they exude are seen as core. Oskar and Patrick had lots of airtime.

Patrick was committed to creating an organization that could consistently deliver on all its promises. We knew we would look at processes, competencies – even structure. But changing the top down culture was where we decided to begin. We knew we needed to get people to feel not only able to resolve issues locally but to feel responsible for it. We would begin with creating new heroes with new stories.

It was a great moment, really. After working together for a few months, a cross-organization team decided that the next all staff meeting would be turned on its head. No top down presentations. The stories would now come from deeper in the organization. New storytellers would get airtime. Oskar and Patrick were all in with the plan.

The stories told that day were new – and true. Everyone started to understand the effort and complexity of auditions – or getting news coverage – or building a rotating set – or arranging a performance in a detention center. They saw the competence and accountability of their peers and saw them as heroes. They used humor. They invited people to drop by. People were visibly excited – and curious – and proud.

The old culture could still be seen in the room as employees repeatedly shifted their gaze back to Oskar and Patrick - making sure they were okay with this new format. What they saw were two leaders totally relaxed and relishing the excellence around them. There was pride and relief on their faces. It was contagious. It was a beginning.

When employees would later go straight to the top, they would be asked, "Have you discussed this yet with (fill in the blank)? The two of you need to figure it out." (Okay, gotta admit. That was just one of the mini-scripts we used to help the execs reinforce the new culture. It still tickles me that we were using scripts in the belly of this amazing theater organization.)

DID YOU HEAR THE ONE ABOUT?

I can't think of anything more deliciously human than being in a room full of people all lost in laughter. For those few minutes we see the folly of things – or the ridiculousness of our habits - together. We can laugh at the hard things in life. We spend most of our time meeting the world's expectations of us. We parent our kids. We do our jobs. We participate in civic or sports or religious or musical activities. Just like everyone around us. And we do it again the next day – and the next.

But sometimes someone can tell a story in just the right way – a story about something so intimate and yet so common - with perfect timing – that we see how vulnerable we all are. Or predictable. Or vain. It strips away our veneer. And we like it.

> "Words are sacred. If you get the right ones in the right order you can nudge the world a little." – Tom Stoppard

Making us laugh is a very special kind of storytelling. With each retelling of the 'joke,' the storytellers notice us as much as we are tuned into them. They patiently find the right sequence and timing – so they can slip into our psyches and give us the surprises we want.

When we humans began living in larger communities, it became immediately clear that we needed to be able to communicate in and with groups – not just with individuals. Whoever developed applause deserves a round of applause. Great innovation.

So it is with laughter – but laughter also plays an important role in our personal lives. Babies start to laugh at 3-months – likely beginning with peek-a-boo. (Nothing seems to be as funny as the unexpected!) And we're hooked. We all – immediately – 'hide' again. Laughter makes us play longer with adults too.

People are more likely to laugh when they are in a group than watching a show alone. The shows aren't funnier – but the social goodwill is contagious. In 1950 the world was introduced to the first laugh track. Just the sound of canned laughter gave TV viewers the experience of being together with people in a live audience. I think canned laughter is like the smiley emoji. It recognizes and touches on our socialness. (It's a real word. I looked it up.)

KING TUT WOULD BE LIKE ANY OTHER 9-YEAR OLD WITHOUT THAT STORY IN HIS POCKET

Over 3500 years ago, young King Tut came to power – and held that power – with a story. Like the Pharaohs before him, and hundreds of kings and queens after him, people were told that God meant for him to be king. Artists created images, myths and symbols that brought the story to life. And with that story came great power.

Although the stories have changed, the power they have is still evident today.

TRUE CONFESSIONS

Okay, it's time for me to 'fess up. I didn't tell you the whole truth in this book. What I shared was true, but – man – I left out a lot. I left out the story about how I self-medicate using Hallmark movies. Or about how much I love parades. I mean I really love parades. I shout thank you to every person marching by. I didn't talk about parades – or Hallmark movies – because they didn't serve my purpose. I selected – edited – with the intention of getting from A to B directly - hoping that you would still like me by the time you finished the book. So – I left out a lot.

If someone asked me about the book I was writing, I changed my story based on how well they knew me – or how involved they were in the arts – or ... Each time I wanted to answer in a way that helped so I told the story a different way.

When people ask us, "Hey, how was your day?" we rarely mention the times we disappointed ourselves or others. Instead we are more likely to tell stories that help people appreciate how hard we worked – or how nice we really are. Because – well – we want to be liked. We don't lie – we just edit. So, you're welcome. This could have been a much longer book.

BRINGING THE CONVERSATION
ABOUT STORYTELLING TO CHILDREN

Young children enjoy language. The magic of stories. Silly rhymes. They see adults happily and easily communicating complex thoughts while they struggle to make the "r" sound.

Scholars have found that hearing and reading stories influence children's understanding of their culture and social rules. They provide safe ways to explore strong emotions and to understand themselves. Science has shown that narratives are deep-rooted in the core of our brain structure, helping us create meaning and relevance, mingling memories with new words and worlds on the page.

CREATE STORYTELLERS BY TELLING STORIES

The intention of this activity is for children to hear you spin a yarn or two. Or tell real anecdotes – in a dramatic way. The magic comes from using something in their real life as the launching point.

Expand your bedtime routine to include 'fresh' stories – stories using something 'real' - stories they can add to in real time. Encourage them to add twists and turns. Take turns beginning. For example:

"When you were just 2 years old, your favorite umbrella looked like a frog. ..." Make up a story about what that special umbrella (shoes, pjs, etc.) did when not in use. Its secret life was very exciting.

"Did I tell you about the time Grandma brought some stars home in her pocket...?"

"Did you know that Fuzzy, your favorite teddy bear, came to me a couple nights ago to tell me a story about the weekend we went away?"

Develop a standard way of winding down until the next bedtime, such as, "and so, we leave this story tonight. We will let those characters go to sleep. Maybe we can revisit them tomorrow?"

OUR BRAIN HAS A SPECIAL POWER: WE CAN READ AND REMEMBER AT THE SAME TIME!

Help your child appreciate that part of the magic of reading or listening to stories is that it is always interactive. Even without trying, when we hear about other worlds or other people, our brains automatically bring our whole selves into the story. We connect it to things that we have known or have felt already - memories. Every now and then, when you are reading a story together ...

"This story is making me remember ..... I'm wondering what sorts of things your brain is bringing into the story right now."

LABEL STORIES

This activity can help your young child learn that written words represent things and that those things can be put together into stories. Use index cards to represent objects in your home. Put the word, "chair" on a chair. Or the words "kitchen chair" or "Mommy's favorite chair" when they are ready for more complexity. Make up some silly cards with mistakes, like a card that says "Mr. Poopy Pants" on their favorite stuffed animal. Have them help you make a correct tag.

Gather a few cards, sit in a comfortable spot, and make up stories using the cards. Have the "stuffed bunny" sit on the "chair" - or "run" - or - ...

LAUNCHING A JOURNALING HABIT

Who says you need to be able to write to keep a journal? With a little help, you can encourage a journaling habit.

Two or three evenings a week, before story time, ask your young child about their day. What did they notice or do or feel? Draw pictures together. Glue special things. Write their words.

JUST 5!

Words matter. After meeting someone – or after an outing or event – or seeing a movie together - you can help your child learn the importance of carefully chosen words. Give everyone a paper and pencil. "In just 5 words, how would you describe ....?" Note the words that match from your lists – and explore those that are different. Anyone want to make changes?

You could make a family game. Everyone has a sheet of paper. Make 5 columns. Select 5 people in your lives. You all have 5 minutes to pick just 5 words that best capture what is special about each person. Compare and enjoy. To expand - you can list favorite television characters.

SPORTS LANGUAGE

These activities can help your child explore the unique demands of storytelling (journalism?) with a sports focus. A genre with its own language and pace. (I have to admit I only understand one word in three when sportscasters do their 'thing.')

Perhaps begin a habit of posting articles on your fridge about your favorite team. Or, when you are watching a game, notice the language and pace. Commit to 'covering' your next meal using the same approach.

Next meal – while cooking – introduce team members with all the energy and hype you heard on TV. "Person #1 is coming up the backfield now – has to find their way to the water pitcher without getting tackled. He's safe!!!!" You get the idea – try to make even the most benign activities sound fantastic. "And the handoff – the pass – the clean up team runs onto the field ..... overcoming the hamstring injury ..."

Provide commentary during a family game of corn hole, horseshoes, rummy.

DOES NONFICTION MEAN TRUE?

These discussion ideas are meant for older children. We all have some basic assumptions about the difference between the literary categories of fiction and non-fiction. But there are so many variations or lenses available when we consider the artistic intentions of both.

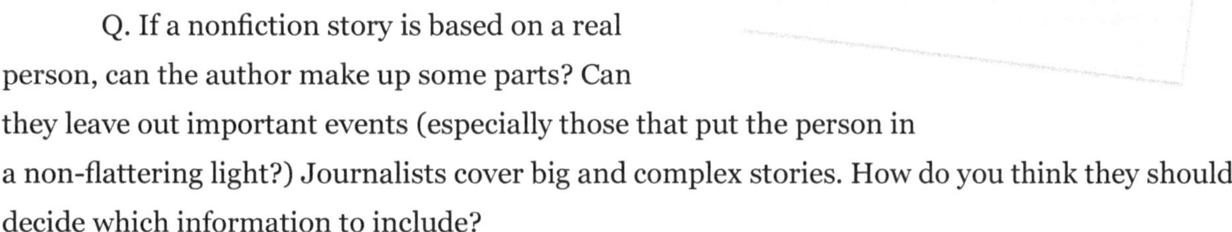

Definitions: Fiction: literature in the form of prose, especially short stories and novels, that describes imaginary events and people. Nonfiction: prose writing that is based on facts, real events, and real people, such as biography or history.

Q. If a nonfiction story is based on a real person, can the author make up some parts? Can they leave out important events (especially those that put the person in a non-flattering light?) Journalists cover big and complex stories. How do you think they should decide which information to include?

A BUDDING AUTHOR IN YOUR MIDST

This activity can set your child onto a path of authorship – as worthy creator. Engage them in creating characters and adventures - and capturing them in their first book(s). Initially it might be easiest to begin with a 'character' in their real world - perhaps a Lego figure - or a Pez container - or something they made out of clay a long time ago.

Q. I think Kitty Pez wants us to write a book about her. She thinks there are other children who would like to hear her story. Before we begin, let's get to know her a little better ourselves. What do you think her favorite song would be? Favorite food? Where does she come from? Does she like to sleep late in the mornings - or wake up early before everyone else?

How old is she? Brothers and sisters? Does she like to laugh? Play sports when we're not around? (The basics of developing a character profile.)

What kind of adventures do we want Kitty Pez to have? Did she have to help rescue another toy? Did she get lost in a big store? No need to write anything yet. Help them develop that imaginary world.

At some point - you get out the paper and begin. Build a book. Be sure to list the author and illustrator on the cover. Invite family members and friends to ask about the book and ask your child to read the story to them. A little magic will happen for your developing author.

CHAPTER 5

APPEARANCE & FASHION

The naked ape – well, more accurately, the rarely naked ape.

First, some facts… The other art forms' power in our lives often reigns under the surface – music heals, inspires and pulls us together. Storytelling stretches our brains and our worlds. Visual arts trigger and challenge. How we 'act' is part of how we grow. But our appearance and fashion? Whoa. Somehow this form of expression and connection turns our insides out. They expose us rather than hide us. For all the world to see. There is no escape. As intended.

Science tells us that we humans, once we ventured out of the shady woods into the savannah, developed an entirely new method of regulating our body temperature. We were still covered with hairs – but they were, generally, tiny rather than thick and fur-like. Our arms and legs got a little longer. We developed new cooling mechanisms and, man, we were off and running. Literally – running. Upright. Through the fields. And cute as hell.

As intended. Of course, with these changes, we had to develop entirely new ways of finding love partners. Standing upright meant that female butts were no longer displaying 'readiness.' Grooming one another, removing bugs and dirt from one another's fur, was no longer an effective socializing technique. Our hairless faces took on much of the communication load. Our features popped with contrasts. The whites of our eyes. Our expressive eyebrows. Our lips got red. Now anyone in the community could read their neighbors for signs of good health or distress or "Come hither" invitations. At the same time our eyes developed a keener ability to distinguish among subtle color shifts. Blushing or puffy red lips could now tell the story.

And, discovery of fire. Ahhh – regulating our body temperatures in the cool evenings around a fire. Perhaps with a good Merlot. Oh, wait. I got lost in the scene for a minute. All this happened over a million years ago. And, still, we didn't seem to have clothing until 150,000 years ago. So that meant that we were running around sans shoes and socks, sans sweatshirts and pajamas, for over 800,000 years! What in hell were we thinking!

Way before then, over 3 million years ago, our species became (basically) monogamous. We mated for life. But that urge – that lust impulse – still lingered. So, when clothing came onto the scene it became de rigueur to keep people's genitals under wraps. Off limits. No more temptation. That would solve the problem. Funny, right?

We humans are nothing if not inventive. I'm thinking bustiers. Muscle shirts. Low-rider jeans. Lipstick. Aviator glasses. Fake eyelashes. Ferraris. Oh wait. Again I forgot where I was. The point is that somewhere along the way, cultures determined that nudity was not okay. And to put muscle behind this expectation they brought out the cultural big gun. Shame.

'Attire' began with woven grasses and hides. Woven flax dates back 36,000 years. Around 5500 BC Egyptians produced linen. Silk was developed in China around 4000 BC. In general we would see lots of draping and wrapping. But in the mid-1300's, around the world, what we think of as clothing made its debut. Form-fitting, curved seams, buttons and laces. And – pose.

Jump to today. Populations have exploded. We live in ever-more crowded communities – literally on top of one another. Our human need to check out our neighbors - to feel safe with one another - to know who has power - to know who does what - has grown ever more challenging and urgent.

Fashion to the rescue. With just a glimpse we can tell a person's gender, age, financial status and maybe even their faith. We can identify law enforcement, doctors, pilots, religious leaders and school crossing guards. We know Rastafarians, monks and military personnel. We can tell the rank and hierarchy in religious orders, military, law enforcement, firefighters and crews working at McDonalds. Just with fabric and color.

> "I'm interested in that whole question of where we wear our identity and how can we see it." –Tilda Swinton

Every morning we put on our identity. Each element sends a message – like Morse code – to like-minded people. "We have something in common." Upper class people can spot one another across a crowded room. They know who is in – and who is wishing they were in. Schools can spot a visiting student easily – the lack of a uniform being an easy giveaway. Sports teams know to throw the ball to others wearing the same uniform.

So – clothing and jewelry and tattoos and hairstyles aren't just on the surface. They mean something. They open a window to our insides.

Let's lift the veil and take a peek at how fashion and appearance plays out in our lives.

WHY DOESN'T GOD WANT TO SEE THE TOP OF MY HEAD?

I could never picture God sitting back on his throne saying, "Hey ladies. Keep that hair covered when you come into my house. Or else." Nor could I picture God saying, as an aside, "Hey guys. We can do whatever we want with our hair. Am I right!? Long or short. Bearded or not. Just don't hide it under a hat!" As a young Catholic girl, these rules never made sense to me.

But I obliged. We all obliged. Most Sundays it was a doily attached with a bobby pin - safely avoiding the hair police another day.

But I get it. Just like football fans want you to know whose team they are on, members of faith communities feel the same. It almost doesn't matter what the rules are – the impulse is the same. We dress to express who we are. And if our faith is core, we want people to know it.

But the thing is, all of these guidelines come from people on earth – people trying to translate basic tenets into tangible representations. And, as with most things, those people – those humans – were influenced by the prevailing customs of their day. Women, generally speaking, don't fare well. In many ways we are all still Eve – making life difficult for the Adams in the world with our bodies. Those tempting bodies – and that, you know, sexy hair.

BODY BULLIES

I'll admit it. It's hard to take compliments.

I was skinny growing up. It wasn't a conscious thing – just the result of an active life. My first year in college changed all that.

Oh, that freshman twenty. Cafeteria food – and lots of it. Vending machines on every floor. All of it served to dull the anxiety. Plus, heck, it was delicious. From that time on, my weight has been up and down – but never quite down enough.

Cultures feel that a person's appearance is within their domain. They define appropriate or acceptable fashion, hair and weight. The closer one hews to the standard, the easier their path will be. That's the reward for compliance. So we spend seemingly endless amounts of money on orthodontists, Botox, teeth whitening, plastic surgery, tanning (or skin lightening), facials, manicures and pedicures, perms and hair

> "They aren't making mirrors like they used to."
> –Tallulah Bankhead

straightening and gym memberships. That's not including our wardrobe, make-up and routine hair maintenance. All to be embraced by our culture. To be liked for the 'individual' (cough cough) we are. (Sorry, I had to clear my throat on that one.)

When people step outside those expectations, the community brings out the enforcement brigade armed with tools of the trade: peer pressure, gossip, shaming and ridicule.

I didn't want my weight to be what my life was about. I was smart. Ambitious. An eager mom. I loved music. Had a hearty laugh. I was a pretty good cook. Overall, I think I was pretty likeable, but ...

There have been so many times in my life when my weight is trending down, that people say to me, with a quick scan of my body from head to toe, "Wow, you look great!" And sometimes, just to be sure I get the message, it is followed up with, "Have you lost weight?"

Point. Match. The world has just taken me by the shoulders and said in its kindest voice – fat is bad. Or worse yet – I was bad because I WAS fat, but now I'm good.

You may not see it on the outside, but I am prickly when it comes to attention to my body. I won't snap at you. I will understand the good intentions even though it can feel like a lion tamer's whip. Control.

If someone is seen as having a 'drinking problem,' people don't feel free to say, "Hey, I noticed you stopped with one glass of wine tonight! Good job!" Or, "Great dental work!" Seriously, we respect the personal nature of those struggles.

We all get messages about our imperfections from marketing and movies and .... the list goes on. But, if we could let it stop there and not have it face us every day in our social and work lives too. Let's limit it to our chosen circle of friends – those who really know and support us.

Now, can you please pass those hors d'oeuvres?

AND THAT'S FUNNY BECAUSE ...?

Okay. We all know that one of the core functions of fashion is to let the community know that we belong – that we aren't a threat. "Nothing to see here – just me – being ordinary – just like you." Humans are built to spot threats – things that are unpredictable – so we can get away – fast.

So – someone long ago thought it would be funny to paint on a crazy face, walk around in giant shoes honking a bicycle horn.

Seriously?

Let me begin by saying I am a Bill Nighy fan. He moves and acts with such glorious ease, dignity and grace. He could be the poster boy for what an unflappable upper class gentleman looks like.

In an interview he said, "When buttoning a three-button jacket, you sometimes button the top one, always the middle, and never the bottom. If you meet a man with the bottom button done up, call a cab. He's not currently functioning—you shouldn't be breathing the same air."

> "Style is about the choices you make to create the aspects of civilization that you wish to uphold." –David Bowie

This is wonderfully tongue-in-cheek, but it also helps us see and understand some basic truths about how our attire sends messages that get us included in or excluded from group cultures. Every group has rules that are required of members. Many of those rules are so subtle that outsiders can miss them entirely – and thus, we inadvertently trip over them. Members know.

THE HOME OF BIAS

Our early years are spent bathed in our family's view of how the world works. As parents, we are in the drivers seat, controlling every aspect (well, almost every aspect) of our kids' lives. From the stories told at the table to our celebrations and rituals. From family heroes to the people we see as threats. All these elements fit together into an integrated worldview. 'This is what I can expect from the world outside my home.'

It's a beautiful thing. Or, at least, it can be a beautiful thing. Sometimes what kids experience in their homes makes them afraid – or super-judgmental – of those outside. They are taught that some people are out to hurt them or take what isn't theirs. In my family, rich people were not to be trusted. In too many homes kids learn that people of a different race or faith are unworthy or even dangerous.

'The Doll Study,' designed in 1939 by psychologists Kenneth and Mamie Clark to explore the effects of racial rejection on children, is a simple but powerful way to see how early bias can take its toll. Their experiment played an important role in convincing the Supreme Court to strike down school segregation in 1952 in the Brown v the Board of Education case. In 2010, CNN commissioned a repeat of the experiment, this time including both black and white children – and the results were strikingly similar. I still can't read it without mourning what we have all lost because of bias.

THE STUDY

Children, ranging in age from three to seven years old, were brought into a room, one at a time, where there were two dolls - identical in every way except their color. One was brown and one was white. They were then asked a series of questions.

- Which is the white doll? Which is the brown doll?

- Which doll is pretty? Which is the ugly doll?

- Which is the nice doll? Why?

- Which is the bad doll? Why?

- Show me the doll you'd like to play with.

The majority of black children ascribed the positive characteristics to the white doll.

After they had answered the questions that basically showed a rejection of the brown doll, they were then asked …

- Which doll looks like you?

The black children looked at the questioner – in pain. Their smiles faded. They didn't want to answer the question. Some even ran out of the room. One boy looked up, smiled and pointed to the brown doll saying, "I'm a n-----, just like him.'

Just think of it. All of the parents of these kids loved them deeply – and wished for the brightest of futures. Just like all of us do. But the cultural messages about race (and other differences) are so pervasive and stealth that they seep into these kids' homes and into their expectations about themselves. We can't close a window to keep them out. They come in through our entertainment, the news, our books, magazines, the conversations at our tables.

I didn't have a busy closet when I was young. It consisted primarily of hand-me-downs from older cousins. Every now and then my Uncle George would come to town, and, like a guardian angel, he would take me downtown to Senter's Department Store to buy me a new dress before he headed back to New Jersey. I didn't worry about clothes anyway. I hadn't learned that yet.

Occasionally parishioners from the church would 'make a donation.' I remember the day when a petite French woman in her fifties, Regine, dropped by our house carrying a light grocery bag. My mom invited her in. She sat quietly at our kitchen table, looking uneasy. She asked me, "Are you going to church regularly?" Yes. "What subjects do you like in school?" Then she stood up and smiled and said, "I think these clothes will look good on you. Be a good girl." She slid the bag toward me and left.

I opened the bag and could immediately see that she had given me clothes from her very own closet. There were silk blouses, a short-sleeved pullover sweater and two knit skirt and jacket ensembles. All just my size. Had I worn them, perhaps with a string of fake pearls, passers-by would have thought I was pretending to be a church lady.

So, even with very little, I knew the risks of dressing out of my norm.

The 'classier' girls in my school would go shopping with their mothers and would learn about fit, cut, style, seasons. They discussed trends and what is proper to wear to a wedding or to camp. I am convinced that having those early conversations set the girls up to notice and to care about all of those elements for the rest of their lives. They developed the ability to read the environment – and match the expectations of the worlds in which they operated. That part of my world was silent.

HOWDY, COWBOY!

A few years ago I had the good fortune of visiting a small town in Oregon where the prevailing culture was – well – cowboy. Residents on horseback routinely rode down the wooden sidewalks. And everyone wore cowboy hats. On day two my mission was to get suited up for where I was. I needed my own hat. Watching the sales associate's eyes as I tried them on gave me guidance. I could see immediately which hats made me laughable – and the one that was 'passable.' I looked like I belonged - kinda. (Actually, I felt like I belonged.) With some last minute guidance on the correct placement, I was out the door and off to the rodeo.

Dressing out of my home culture felt odd and wonderful. There were moments when, tucking my thumbs into my pockets and swaggering over to that there bakery, I thought, "THIS is it. This is who I was meant to be!" Some parts of me got 'lit' for a while, like taking off a shroud or an ill-fitting mask. I kicked the dust off my boots (okay, sandals) hopped into the open Jeep, and rode off into the sunset.

POWER OF A UNIFORM – PART ONE

Imagine this. A member of a winning high school basketball team was seen drinking at an unchaperoned party – wearing his team jacket. A photo was posted on social media with the caption, "Go team!"

Wearing a uniform is no simple gesture. It's a commitment to the team (or organization) and a promise to uphold its values – at least while on the job. One kid's actions can affect the reputation of the team, the coach and even the other team members.

When kids get onto their first team, they embark on a lifelong learning journey working the boundaries between me and we. Responsibilities to the sport – and to each other – go way beyond learning how to pass and dribble. Even 'stars' start to see themselves as one of – learning to celebrate the 'we' instead of the 'me.' Letting team members down for the first time can be traumatic – and motivating. Finding the courage to get back in there is really tough.

> "Clothes make the man. Naked people have little or no influence on society."
> –Mark Twain

And it is all sealed with the public donning of the team uniform. For all to see.

I think a major turning point, the point at which our class systems became amplified, was when Maslow, in 1943, introduced his theory about human's hierarchy of needs. It suggests that people are motivated to fulfill basic needs before moving on to other, more advanced needs. After meeting our biological needs like food, water and sleep – and then our safety needs – like predictability, shelter, routine – we all then turn to our need to be connected to those around us. Our need to belong.

Marketing departments could sell us almost anything if we believed it would make us more likable. More handsome. More fun. More – classy. Ah – that handsome macho Chesterfield Man. The shapely woman in her apron just glowing because her bathroom bowl is sparkling. Fast cars. Face creams. Fashion. Just make us consumers feel less than – make us feel not-good-enough unless we looked like this, or smelled like this or cooked like Betty Crocker.

Our culture is both reflected and reinforced by all those ads.

The finely groomed men in tailored suits wearing expensive watches – in front of expensive cars. The message is, "I have my act together. I am financially independent. I am king of the jungle." Those same ads often show women draped over the hood of the car wearing dramatic and somewhat revealing fashion, hair that flows, red lips, diamonds sprinkled everywhere. The message? "Do you want to be in the company of a woman like this? Drive this car – this very expensive car – and they will come your way.

These sorts of ads are selling status, giving us all an understanding of what exclusivity looks like. If we want to belong, here's what we need to do. Just try to look away.

"Culture war – the struggle between social groups for dominance of their values, beliefs, and practices."

In the early U.S., Americans had an Indian problem. Their belief in manifest destiny (that this whole continent was destined to belong to the white Europeans) magnified the challenge. All the indigenous peoples were in the way. They tried removing them (Trail of Tears), initiated when the people of Georgia wanted the gold that was in Indian territory. They tried military dominance, ending with Custer's efforts. Then, the nearly fatal blow, came with efforts to kill their spirit and their culture. Those things that defined Native American identity.

The Carlisle Indian Industrial School. One of the most brutal weapons in this culture war was initiated by a Civil War veteran, Capt. Richard Henry Pratt, who convinced the government to fund Indian boarding schools. Mandatory assimilation. The Carlisle Indian Industrial School in Pennsylvania was the first of hundreds of publicly run institutions, supported by hundreds more run by Christian charities. Children taken from the reservations were given new names, haircuts, a new language, stories, history and food. They were stripped of their native clothes and other adornments. They were not only forbidden to speak their own language (and punished when they slipped up), but any reminders brought from home were ceremoniously burned. The life they knew – the families left behind – were presented as shameful.

The driving idea was to make them real Americans. Although they might resist initially, they would eventually appreciate all the benefits coming their way. This land of opportunity. All they had to do was look and act like us. Simple, right?

The cycle of destruction intensified as Native Americans were forced onto smaller and smaller reservations devoid of opportunity – and hope. The freedom, culture and community that had defined their way of life were replaced with dependence, shame and despair. When children would return home after nine months in assimilation schools, looking, acting and speaking like the white man, you can only imagine how their parents felt. And the kids? Well they had been receiving a steady diet of criticism of the Native way of life. Many families fell apart.

One boy, who had experienced extreme punishment over instinctively using his native tongue, just fell apart when he returned to his family. He couldn't remember his own language. His parents held him close – and kept him home. He later said, as he was trying to reconnect with his heritage and identity, "I tried to reconnect with our spirits, but they didn't understand English." As a man now in his 60's, he wept retelling the story. "I lost my voice."

Cultures only survive through their children. Native Americans were denied that. As recently as 1967, the Bureau of Indian Administration and the Child Welfare League of America encouraged adoption of Native American children by non-Native families. In 1978 (yes, that's right, 1978), close to 35% of all Native American children were removed from their homes.

VIDAL SASSOON IN THE MAINE WOODS

In the summer of '66 I went to work at a small resort on Rangeley Lake in northern Maine. There were about 20 small cabins and an inn. Most of the patrons came up from the big cities just to get away from the hustle and bustle for a while - for some peace and quiet and nature. I was primarily responsible for serving and tending all their kids during mealtime while the adults enjoyed their dinner in the main dining room. The rest of the time I was there to help in whatever ways I could.

One day I was sitting on the dock after going for a swim with two of the children from New York City. Their mother came and sat next to me, slipping off her sandals and dipping her feet into the water. She asked me about my life. What I wanted to do. She told me how much her kids liked me and how much she appreciated that. "Have you ever heard of Vidal Sassoon?" she asked. No. "Well I work in his salon in NYC. It's kind of a fancy place." Oh, nice. "I know you're going away to school next month. Would you like me to give you a nice haircut to help you get ready?" I smiled and looked down. I knew it was important not to 'put her out' – to make her work in any way. She said, "How about this. You run up and take a shower and meet me at my cabin. I'll be all ready for you on the porch." I smiled – and obliged.

I had never had a professional cut like this. Everything about it felt special. The way she carefully combed my hair and parted it into sections. She had big silver clips. She snipped away then stepped back and smiled at me. "Well, if you don't look like you belong on the cover of a magazine, Susie."

It was such a loving and generous act. But here's the thing. That summer Vidal Sassoon was all the talk because of his revolutionary asymmetrical styles. I can still see images of Twiggy in my mind sporting her blonde version. Instead of looking like a church lady in someone else's clothes I was now sporting a haircut from a class and region that was not my own. My family thought it was laughable when I got home. Ahhh – the challenges of good intentions.

GENDERED SHOES?

Have you ever held up a sandal you liked and asked, "Is this a men's or women's sandal?" The truth is it is hard to tell – but we feel it is important to know. They aren't like shirts. It's easy to tell with shirts. They button on opposite sides.

What to do. Oh, what to do.

POWER OF A UNIFORM, PART TWO: SPECIAL POWER

Most cultures and communities identify people who have power over other members of their group. The protectors. The rule keepers.

Once I left a picnic blanket on a section of grass in Central Park while I sauntered down to the amphitheater to watch the roller skaters – roller dancers really. When I got back, still on a bit of a high from all the music, there was a woman – and older woman with a duck-brimmed hat and a clipboard – coming up to me with her finger wagging. "You need to pick up that blanket now. Don't you know that you ruin the grass by leaving it there all afternoon!"

> "I like to move fast, and wearing high heels was tough, and low heels with a skirt is unattractive. So pants took over."
> –Katherine Hepburn

Uhhhh. Of course my instinct was to apologize, to thank her for pointing that out. But soon I thought, "Who are you? What gives you the power to tell me what to do?!"

That is a serious question for anyone living in a community. A very serious question.

Some people actually do have that power because the community has authorized them to have that power – to act on behalf of the greater whole. Their job is to intervene when community rules are broken and, in some cases, to temporarily take away our individual freedom. To stop the offense.

Fashion challenge, right? How are members of a community supposed to know who has that real power so they can trust their orders? Not sure if, "Sir, I didn't know that was a police officer," would carry much weight.

There can be absolutely no room for doubt.

So – I'm thinking that if that bossy park lady every approaches me again I might say, "Oh yeah? Show me your badge," as I humbly and quietly move my blanket to a new spot.

FALL FROM CUTE

God – how we set little girls up for the inevitable fall from cute. From the time the pink name card is displayed in the hospital nursery, their role description is clear. We love to frame their lives in pink, in ruffles, in sweet. Why do we yield so completely to this ritual? "So cute." "So pretty." It's the first thing – and often the only thing – that warrants comment from every adult she meets. After all, we couldn't say "you're so smart," could we? We can't see smart so we applaud what we can see.

> "Fashion offers no greater challenge than finding what works for night without looking like you are wearing a costume." –Vera Wang

Of course this attention to cute finds its way into a young girl's sense of who she is – of why she feels valued.

But get beyond the cute stage and into awkward, or into utilitarian haircuts (they have to be ready for school after all) or the gender-neutral apparel of primary school – and what happens? Adults' eyes no longer show excitement. "But hey I'm good at math." Great. We really mean that –

but our delight is now tempered, logical. How can they get back to that magic feeling?

The media will show them how. Instead of living for families' eyes to light up, they now look to the broader community for approval. Hot becomes the new cute.

SNIDELY? IS THAT YOU?

I took a seat at the bar at Mulherin's. It was my first visit. I had lived in Fishtown, a suburb of Philadelphia, for a while and was, frankly, starved for characters in my life. While in New York City, I felt I was never more than a greeting away from meeting someone new – and interesting. People with stories to tell. But I had yet to develop my spidey-sense on where to find those people in my new neighborhood.

And then the bartender, Scott, welcomed me with a glass of water and a menu. Yep, it was like someone just put a good book in front of me. Well. Well. What have we here!

Scott was a playwright and actor who was into … well, what wasn't he into! We talked about Jodororosky, contemporary theater, the occult, history, astrology, wine. Lots of wine talk. At the bar, over the course of a year he took me on an Amaro tour, teaching me the subtleties and joy in that bitterness scale. He had tattoos. A gravelly growley voice. A hearty laugh. But with all that, the feature that was most pronounced – most in my face – was his Snidely Whiplash mustache.

When people's eyes would get stuck on his mustache, he would sometimes point his fingers at it and then raise them up to his eyeballs saying, "I'm up here." Such an interesting tension.

I asked Scott to share some thoughts on his mustache journey.

How did the mustache begin? "Just before I left New York I had a few months where I was only doing theater work in a workshop space. It was the first time since my youth that I hadn't been required to maintain some sort of 'professional' appearance for a job. I stopped shaving.

When it was long enough, I began to twist the ends – as a joke. I thought it was funny – absurd. But, by the end of that week I realized I actually liked it."

Imagine that tomorrow morning you woke up and it was totally gone. "Actually people make this joke with me a lot that they're going to cut it off in my sleep. I've had dreams where something horrific happens to my mustache and then I have to suddenly go bare-faced. I suppose at this point, over seven years in, there's a bit of attachment to my identity.

But - I'm performing soon in a Sam Shepard play and have already signed a contract saying that I'll change my hair and appearance as requested. It may be gone soon."

Do mustaches send any kind of message? "Some people took mine as an immediate sign that I'm clearly an asshole. And they tell me so."

Having this discussion with Scott reminded me of how bossy cultures can be – how people in a culture feel it is their right – perhaps even their duty – to intervene or shame aspects of our identity they don't feel are appropriate. Perhaps we could all use a script – let's get a new script – to respond.

A SEA OF CHANEL SUITS

Conferences and networking. Two words that always filled me with dread. I barely fit into the fashion expectations in any single organization – marginally passing the good-enough test – but events with crowds of savvy suited women all at once? Ack. I always felt exposed.

While I was in New York City working at Chase Bank, I was invited to join an all-women's HR Executives group - a networking group. My role, leading the Organizational Development and Change Management functions, was always tangential to what were considered the prime HR disciplines – payroll, employee relations, recruiting, benefits. So there wasn't a lot of exciting overlap that could drive good conversations. But I appreciated the invitation and committed to trying to get better at blending.

We met for drinks and dinner every few weeks. As they all chatted around the table wearing their Chanel suits, their highish heels and their poufy hair, there would be occasional discussions about work. I was surprised that most of the energy went into more personal topics. The best place to get your hair done. The best bath salts. Where they were going on vacation. They would twinkle their fingers for the group to see their nail color.

These were all very competent executives. But these evenings were actually exercises in class and status. They were all lovely toward me but it was clear that I was from another world. I was a duck at a table of swans.would twinkle their fingers for the group to see their nail color.

BRINGING THE CONVERSATION
ABOUT APPEARANCE TO CHILDREN

They have so little choice, really. In their early days we decorate our children as we choose. Eventually it starts to matter to them – a lot. Favorite colors. T-shirts. Boots with ducks on them. Some prefer no clothes at all. We can help our young learners, still unaware of the pressure that will soon follow, understand the basic elements of clothing. Expose the wizard before he can take control.

When kids start school, they are in a demanding life skills lab. In the safety of family, they are loved and celebrated, whatever they do. But now, in the school environment, there are new rules. Looks take center stage. It becomes clear to them that, if they want to be liked and to belong, they need to pay attention to what the other children are doing. Being different has its costs.

SCHOOL FASHION

This conversation/game will help your child appreciate that clothing matters – a lot. (It won't be news to them.) It will also help them understand all the components that people see – and judge. People 'read' each others' clothing to learn about their values or family income or even favorite musical genres. It can also marginalize or isolate kids.

What Is Most Important About What You Wear (at School)?

Make up cards listing criteria. Some suggestions: fits well; everyone else is wearing something like it; new; expensive brand; clean; modest; (utility) supports the activity you're doing; don't keep wearing the same thing; other ideas? Ask your child to put these in order of importance. Do they think others would order them the same way?

Other conversation ideas: What if someone had new clothes that didn't really fit? Why might that happen? What if someone wears the same clothes over and over again? Why might that happen? Are there kids at school who follow any extreme trends? What do you think they might be saying? Do some kids get teased about what they wear?

Brainstorm a list of what you CAN'T tell about a person based on what they are wearing?

Watching a TV show together gives you an opportunity to raise awareness of the role of fashion/costume in defining characters.

"Why do you think the the costume designers for this show (movie, TV and animation) decided on the main characters' appearance?"

HAIRSTYLES SHOW BELONGING

Explore differences between styles for men and women. Explore ways people make their styles unique.

Why do you think they evolved that way?

What do people's hairstyles tell us about the groups they belong to?

Why do you think trends keep changing?

Do any kids get teased for how they wear their hair?

EXPLORING THE OUCH IN FASHION

We all want to be loved and appreciated. Clothing sends messages about our gender, faith, social status, ethnicity, favorite teams or musicians ... the list goes on. Sometimes these rules get defined for us. For example, for centuries in China women bound their feet to keep them small – because small feet were considered beautiful. In the western world, corsets squeezed the breath out of women so they could meet society's expectations for a small waist.

Together explore ways that people today put up with some discomfort in order to make a 'fashion statement.' (Ex: High heels, jeans worn so low they are about to fall off, body piercings, facial waxing, tanning, hair straightening, cosmetic surgery, skin lightening.)

FASHION IDENTIFIERS

The purpose of these discussion ideas is to help your child understand the role clothing plays in important roles and ceremonies in life. Clothing adds solemnity and serves to indicate special stature. They let us live - peacefully - in large communities.

A priest recognized that those "clothes are not just about me, they are about my relationship with everyone out there. When I wear that black clerical shirt in public, when I pull that white tab across my throat, I am giving myself to them. The people I encounter then, they no longer see the 'me' I'd like them to see…Instead, they see 'priest.'"

CHAPTER 6

IN PRAISE OF ARTISTS ALL AROUND ME

I'm sure it is clear by now that I see art everywhere. Expressions of identity - of belonging - of understanding and interpretation. All of it fuels our connection to - or separation from - the people around us. We are bathed in the arts. They form and reinforce our social structures, beliefs and traditions. They bring meaning and relevance.

This chapter shifts that focus from the impact of the arts in our lives - to the creators. To the artists themselves. Specifically - artists I have known. People whose voices I know. People who did their shapeshifting right in front of me - transitioning from the friend to the performer. To the giver.

I hope you enjoy getting to know them.

I wanted to begin this book journey by going to the source. To the beginning. Might I actually be able to speak with Art directly since she has been such a powerful force in my life? I knew it wouldn't be easy but, damn, it was worth a try, right?

There was no website to explore. She wasn't on LinkedIn. But I eventually found someone who knew someone who agreed to lob my request for an interview into the Art universe. After a few emails back and forth, she finally agreed to meet with me. The turning point came when she realized that I wanted to show her as the workhorse she really is – to show all the brains and brawn. The heavy lifting.

We agreed to meet for a late lunch at Lafayette Restaurant. A table outside would be good - though I worried that passers-by might recognize her and interrupt our precious interview time.

"Without art, we should have no notion of the sacred."
–W. H. Auden

But that wasn't a worry. She showed up in overalls, her grey hair pulled back with a clip - so she went unnoticed. Relatively. New Yorkers know how to give celebrities their space.

"Thanks for agreeing to meet with me. I really hope I can get people to see the other side of all you do. To see that you're not just a pretty face."

"Yeah. Yeah. I get it. But I have to tell you, there are thousands – no – hundreds of thousands – of books out there already. Supposed biographies. 'Isn't this beautiful! Isn't this creative! Blah. Blah. Blah.' Honestly I wanted to say to every one of them, "Hey! I'm busy keeping the world running here!"

I couldn't have loved her more than I did right then. She was impatient, brilliant, accustomed to fame – and over it. There would be no messing around.

She lit one of those cigarettes that looks like a little cigar – took a few puffs – then leaned in so close that I could smell the history on her breath – or maybe it was the cigarette. "They don't get it. They think my work is just in galleries, libraries and performance halls. "And they just looove to critique. Was I successful or not!' But what I want the world to know – and what I am counting on you to tell them – if they want to see me – the real me – they should look at an effin

brain scan. THAT'S where they'll find my best work."
She sat back and looked off to the side. When she
turned back, we both started laughing.

"Can you tell me about how you got started?"

"Sure. It may have been a million years ago
but I remember it like it was yesterday. Mother
Nature and I – well, we took on the challenge
of taking those early cavemen (They were a bit
doltish.) and turning them into something special.
"What if we made these guys the best builders and
the best organizers in the animal kingdom? Give
them the power of one by making them hungry to connect
and work together? THAT could really change the evolutionary landscape, right?"

Our sandwiches came and Art ordered another wine spritzer.

"So – what did you do?"

"Well, we went into the lab, of course. We kept asking, 'what could we do to make getting
along easier?' Or, 'If they're going to be in groups a lot of the time, how can they all communicate
at the same time?' You know, questions like that. Then we'd each come up with some ideas and
we'd play them out. It was a puzzle though. Our first tries – well – humans would have needed a
brain the size of a house. So, little by little we found ways to build in multitasking. But, at the end
of the day – I think our collaborations have survived the test of time. Look at us – sitting here
reading menus, having a good laugh together. By the way – laughter? That was my idea. I just
had a sense that, if people could tell stories in ways that made others laugh … well it would be like
putting down their weapons, don't you think?"

"Um – yah. Of course."

She reached into her back pocket and pulled out her wallet. "Here, let me show you a
picture of what Mo and I came up with – our baby." There was brain image after brain image
labeled with complex names and functions. "See that part there – the color thing? That was all me.
I had to fight hard to build responses to color in there – it took some finagling. But – man – it paid
off, right?"

"So – it sounds like you and Mother Nature were – close."

She gave me a wink. "You betcha. For a while there we couldn't get enough of each other. We felt – powerful. The sky was the limit."

"Are you still together?"

"Well, you know. We have to get the old band together every now and then. Create some new music for the world." She started packing up – like she was getting ready to leave.

"Can I ask you just a couple more quick questions?"

She set her bag back down. "Sure, honey. What have you got?"

"Anything you regret?"

"Mimes. We should have thought that one through a little more. Good concept – but – what do you do with it?"

"Favorites? Superstars you really appreciated?"

"Ooooo, yes. That guy Caraveggio! Such an asshole – but he totally changed how people related to their religion. He showed it in dark streets and dirty hands. You know, like in real life. Art with a job to do - to persuade the masses."

"Real life. I like that phrase. Can I use it?"

"It's yours. And everyone else's too. Just go for it."

"Sorry – I interrupted you. Any other faves?"

"Ah – yes. Oliver Sachs. That guy – well – he put that art/science overlap to work. It seemed like magic to people. Mo and I were so proud that day – proud that one of our creations – music – was getting the credit it deserved." She smiled and said, "Hey, you want to see a picture of where music lives in the brain?"

"Very funny," I said. "It's everywhere, right?"

"Yes – but I have to show you anyway." She flipped out a rotating image of a brain with waves of rainbow colors pulsating across the surface. "Pretty great, right?"

She picked up her bag again, put her hand on my arm. "Give it a try. I'm with you. It's not going to be an easy sell but it could be a fun trip just trying."

"Thanks so much. And will you send my regards to Mother Nature too?"

"You can count on it." And away she went.

I think I remember all of this. Or maybe it was a dream.

ELIZABETH STREB

Oh my. I almost need a seatbelt to tell the story.

I had seen Elizabeth at The Noho Star – a favorite breakfast spot for many in the art world. Like people do in New York City (maybe in every city, I don't really know) over time we started exchanging greetings, then a stand-by-the-table good-by. Til, eventually we agreed to meet. Early conversations were about the arts – and arts funding specifically which seems to be the bane of so many artists' existence.

Eventually we delved in a little deeper – about what fascinates her. About how far or how big she could take ideas. About balancing risk and concept. About gravity and flight. About circus.

The Noho Star closed for good. We were all bereft. Over the course of the next few weeks we all begrudgingly scattered ourselves like marbles on a table top – finding new spots – making new friends. And then I moved to Philly. A year later Elizabeth and I arranged to meet for breakfast at Lafayette.

"When I'm writing a new play, there's a period where I know I shouldn't be out in public much. You willfully loosen some of the inner straps that hold your core together." – Tony Kushner

We both talked about what was on our minds – getting caught up. Then she went to that place where artists go - here but not really here. Suddenly it was like I was watching a documentary of an artist/genius at work. (For those of you who are unfamiliar with Elizabeth's work, she was a winner of the MacArthur genius grant.) She started sketching the components of an idea but instantly felt the constraints of the paper in front of her. How to capture the motion – and dimension? She lifted one page. Folded another. She did instant - and complicated - calculations about weight, height, motion, torque. She'd turn it and explain the action. 3D – then 4D. As she wove in other elements the pace picked up – like a freight train right there at the table. I swear I saw her ducking and weaving – living on that page.

Forever grateful.

DAVE MALLETT

The Chocolate Church in Bath was something like a holy place for me when I went to work there in 1980. For two glorious years I had the privilege of serving artists, patrons and audience members in equal measure.

> *"I'm restless. Things are calling me away.*
> *My hair is being pulled by the stars again."*
> *—Anais Nin*

I constantly mingled with people whose bodies and minds were being offered up in service of their talent. Like stewards of something the community needs. Later in life I would come to appreciate how, when voices fade or mastery weakens, the audience moves on. It was the talent they wanted all along – not the vehicle. It is a fragile ecology. And I was there – in awe and appreciation.

For a week Dave Mallett and his band had been preparing to do two live weekend concert recordings. He was always quiet, reserved. Kind. When I told him I was really looking forward to hearing *Fire*, he smiled. Of course, as luck would have it, house management details took over and I had to miss both shows. As the last of the audience was filing out I walked up the center aisle applauding. He gave a grin and asked if I had been there for *Fire*. I dropped my head and said I was so sorry – but, no. I had missed it.

He invited me to have a seat in the front row of the now empty theater and asked his band to "C'mon back up" to the stage. "This one is for Susan."

Dave was standing at the front of the stage. His mic – now dead – was behind him. He smiled at me and began to strum – and then sing. But within a just few seconds he backed himself up and sang the rest of the song into that quiet mic – safely suited up. I think I had seen the turtle outside his shell.

I was overcome with appreciation for his – and other performers' bravery. To play against type. To do what is inherently uncomfortable so the gift can be given.

TORI SCOTT

I think my Tori Scott story is the classic NYC artist story. Artists are everywhere – barely hanging on, working a day job or two for the privilege of getting one more audition. One more gig. One more chance.

I was at The Public Theater when I met Tori. She was working in the development department that was about to undergo a major restructuring. Although it was never officially talked about, people knew. People always know - as they should.

Part of the prep is to spend time with the major players getting familiar with their ambitions, talents and options. Tori wanted a very specific position – and one that we both understood would likely go to someone else with more experience. The prospect of not getting into the new structure didn't seem to bother her. I was curious.

We were sitting in Oskar's office in an old leather couch that we actually sat down into – bringing our knees up to our chins. But, hey, it was private.

"So, Tori. Talk to me about other things you would like to do if this position doesn't happen for you."

She quietly said, "I want to sing. I think I would really give it a shot this time."

Shame on me for doubting – but hey – I hadn't yet heard her sing. Just before the department made the changes, she had a gig at Joe's Pub. The rest, as they say, is history.

From the first note, I was stunned. A diva voice with Bette Midler humor. She could jump from tender to bawdy in an instant. The packed house was in her hands. I felt more than a little humbled. Damn – that keeps happening to me. And I love it.

Michael was a successful composer and lyricist who worked on and off Broadway. His role at The Public Theater meant that he spent a lot of time in our midst. Always engaging. Ready to agree or disagree – with vigor. Shortly after Donald Trump took office, Michael and I were in a borrowed office when I expressed my concern about the arts losing funding. He looked down at the floor for a while then smiled and assured me, "Susan, as long as people are on this earth, some of us will want to get dressed up to entertain and perform. For free. Don't worry."

> "The poet judges not as a judge judges but as the sun falling around a helpless thing."
> —Walt Whitman

Michael died just a few months later at 41.

BLUE MAN GROUP

In 1991 my daughter was in her first year at Barnard College so I jumped at any reason to make the trip to NYC. I was still living in Maine, working at L.L.Bean. One Sunday morning one of those moments happened where life was about to take a turn and I didn't know it. I saw a television segment about a new performance group making big waves in NYC - Blue Man Group. Chris Wink was interviewed - already in bald cap - getting himself blue. He was clever and witty as he explained the concepts of the show. Seeing clips of the music and the mayhem - I just knew I needed to partake. Within an hour I had purchased two tickets.

I couldn't have imagined that just a few short years later I would have the privilege of working with Blue Man Group as they opened a second show in Boston, then another in Chicago - and beyond. This suddenly-expanded organization needed structure, strategy, job descriptions, documented processes, etc. - the Plymouth Rock of OD. Chris, Matt and Phil were brilliant, creative, intense, collaborative - uninhibited. Every idea contained equal parts art and science. They were deliberate about where in our bodies the music would land. They took us on multimedia excursions into eye structure and big city sewer systems. (Arrows showing the contents going "away" - still makes me laugh.) The science of marshmallows and Cap'n Crunch. And the visual dynamics of paint drumming. And …

At the core of the characters, though, was their role as shamans - inviting us all into this new kind of community - this innocent, silly community. The Blue Men seemed almost like pastors as they maintained eye contact with the audience - relating, finding the energy, helping us focus. There was no fourth wall.

Their work both on and off the stage continues to inspire - and make me laugh. So grateful.

MEMBERS OF SUMMER BANDS IN EVERY CITY PARK

Sometimes it's the things closest to us – things that are so embedded in routine and expectations that we barely notice the difference they make in our lives. So it is with summer bands. Unsung heroes.

We wander into the park with our toddlers carrying folding chairs for grandma and grandpa. We find a space and spread out the blankets and unpack the snacks for the evening. A bag holds extra sweaters. If we are in Maine, bug spray is a must. But we settle in. As soon as the music begins the magic starts to happen. The littlest kids – perhaps still in diapers – start the show. They get a good strong stance and then start to bounce. And bounce. When they feel confident they look around (while bouncing) – and see a crowd of loving eyes – so they bounce even more. Preschool kids run and dance. Playing is different when music fills the air. And marches – well they are actually irresistible.

Together all these people will hear Broadway tunes, marches, old spirituals, big band sounds, some oldies and fresh takes on popular music. When some of the older songs are played, grandparents will remember when – and tell the kids how important that song was to them so long ago.

By the time the concert is over, the kids' music vocabulary will have grown. When else in their routines do they hear "It's a Grand Ole Flag," "The A Train" and "Somewhere Over the Rainbow?" When else can they move – fly – to the music so freely? Or hear a silly trombone or maracas and gongs? Some might even fall asleep.

This is the gift. Peace. Play. Wrapped in a community. Compliments of the band. When we enjoy a song all together, the walls between us actually go down. And we can be lifted together.

Music on the grass. Thank you, summer bands.

A few evenings ago I was enjoying dinner at the bar of a favorite (high-end-ish) restaurant. The bartender, a Kennedy-esque, studied, master-engager – I'll call him James – was doing what bartenders do best – spinning the powers of spirits, alchemy and collective goodwill. At

one point in this evening he did what he had done hundreds of times, but this time it was different. He mixed two cocktails, banged them into their shakers then proceeded to do a nice 'hard shake.' Slight taps to open ... and ... boom ... the entire restaurant spontaneously burst into applause. A feeling of appreciation raced through everyone there. Appreciation for James and his colleagues, Appreciation for the shared moment, the shared rituals. I know it sounds corny but – appreciation to be alive and in company.

Bartenders are master performers of ceremony and rituals. The greetings. The settings. The 'How are you today's?', 'Here, let me get that for you.' ,'How is everything?', followed by a smile and an add on comment or two to show they know exactly what you mean. In other words, validating what you have said. The way to display a bottle of wine as they discuss its profile. The tasting. The evening is a series of respectful gestures. Everyone deserves that at the end of a day, do they not?

Shaman. If you look up the meaning you often see terms such as 'healing' or 'energy' or 'access to the spirits of good and evil.' Shamans can conjure up the forces – the spirits – of a community and put them to work for good. Aren't bartenders the same? They meet people where they are, help them unhinge from all that's going on 'out there.' When people feel seen and respected, the walls come down. People relax and start to see one another – to reach out to one another. Plus – it's almost ridiculously dead-on that they serve spirits. It's like the room gets bathed in good will for one another. It seems we were in good hands.

Cheers!

This shouldn't have taken me by surprise – but it did. It wasn't that I had low expectations. It was more like I was suddenly exposed to how much more there can be to a performer – or a genre – than I had come to expect. I thought I knew more than I did.

One afternoon in Joseph, Oregon I was invited by a friend to attend a concert by a musician at the local arts center. There were maybe a dozen people in attendance spread out among thirty folding chairs. Of course I was thrilled to find a seat right up front – within inches of the performer. Opportunities like that never happened in NYC. A bearded young man, Forrest Von Tuyl, with scuffed boots and calloused hands walked out and quietly sat on a stool just a few feet from me. He didn't make much conversation. He just began to play. Over the course of the next hour he told us of his life in the outdoors – higher up the mountain. About hard work. Life without any of the conveniences most of us think of as essential. And yet he saw beauty.

He sang about grit and love and life. His voice was a combination of gravelly and tender. His words – well his words stunned me with their poetry. I kept looking to my neighbors – wanting to say, "Are you hearing this? Isn't this beautiful? Isn't he wonderful?" He referenced Goethe and Shakespeare. And he sang the words, "Like lightning striking a barbed wire fence."

That vivid crackling image still stuns me to this day. It captures what art is in my life. Thank you, Forrest.

Like lightning striking a barbed wire fence.

MY JONAH AND THE WHALE EXPERIENCE

Into the belly ....

It was surreal and hyper-sensory at the same time. I was standing in the small entry of The Performing Arts Center at Bath – the Chocolate Church - amidst eight members of a Scottish Bagpipe band. Just the other side of the doors was a full house quietly anticipating the familiar sound. How artists enter and begin their performances is always important. On this evening, the band wanted the audience to hear first – then see.

There I was tangled in the squeezing arms, the breathing bags and the whispering pipes. Art filling every inch of a space. I was appreciating the science of the bagpipe technology and design, and its history and its knock-you-to-the-floor emotional punch. I was in awe of the players – and their histories and their years of practice and their goodwill. And those kilts and storied plaids and tassled socks. The tending – the slow aspirations they all practiced to keep those instruments ready to wail as the doors are opened. Looking into each other's eyes –a wink, a wide-eye, a slow blink – staying aligned and ready. It was all there. In compressed time. In ensemble. I was physically and emotionally breathing in art and culture. It was physical force – so much more than an auditory one.

I have been fortunate in my life. Many blessings along the way. But I think I am most grateful for those exquisite moments when I can be with artists as they begin. When they make that leap from being like you and me into that giving place – that selfless place. When they put themselves into the service of their art or their truth. It is like a flash – a quick last bit of eye contact – then – the performer takes the lead. The transformation is complete.

TONY AT THE BAR

I was at one of my favorite spots, the bar at Mulherin's, enjoying the good vibe and interesting people. To my left I met Christine, a visual artist who had heard Janis Joplin at the Monterey Pop Festival in 1967, and her husband Tony. At one point I said, "Tony, I like your hat. And has anyone ever told you that you have a great voice?"

"The hallmark of an artist is generosity."
–T Bone Burnett

And then he told me the story. He had been, for a few years, listed in Ripley's Believe It or Not for hitting the lowest note known to humans. He had sung in barbershop quartets and had been in a chorus at Carnegie Hall. He then sang for me – *Summertime*. On the spot. Side by side. Like the low rumble of a bear. Amazing.

Life is so good.

IN CLOSING

"Without art, we should have no notion of the sacred." –W. H. Auden

This book has been a journey for me. A journey back into those stunning moments when art / artist have changed my life - given it depth, richness and connection.

But this chapter - this look at the artists themselves - means even more to me. At the core of every story was an individual that I came to know - even if just a little. An enthusiastic or weary or ambitious or tender individual who generously let me in. They talked about their ideas and how they were going to try one more time. For some - even in the face of great success - the work stayed hard. Some battled the public's expectations for more of the same. I knew some on their way up and some who were hanging up their tools. I got to see their creations, their vulnerabilities, their diligence and doggedness. Their bravery. Mostly - their bravery.

At one point I considered naming this book "Superfan" because I am endlessly grateful to the artists in our world. Sit two of us at a performance at a small venue – and one of us will be appreciating – maybe smiling and nodding to the rhythm. The other? Me? Well, I will be using all my strength not to shout thank you. I will be the one leaning into my fellow audience members and asking, "Wow! Isn't that great?!" Or turning to the person next to me in a gallery - looking to share what is happening for me. It is almost impossible for me to be alone in those moments.

As intended. In 2012 Captain and Tennile sang, "Art will keep us together!" Or maybe I was hearing it wrong. Perhaps they said "Love." If so - they misspoke.

ACKNOWLEDGEMENTS

Oh, so many people have helped me get this book to the finish line. Let me name just a few.

Jen Wink Hays (my daughter)

Jen, you get the Artistry and Feedback Award. You understood my mission as it lived in my head and heart. I could always count on you to shoot straight - to give not-so-easy feedback when necessary. From paragraphs that didn't work to visual stories that could improve - you kept me on my toes. Your graphic design roots - like magic - gave me the pegboard cover concept that tickles me still. Your influence is everywhere. Thank you.

The Team at LTL MTN

You get the James Beard-Equivalent Award for working with a seemingly endless array of ingredients and turning them into something delicious. Steve Koester - you brought strategy, structure and marketing chops - with a steady diet of inspiration. When I could barely lift my head up to listen, you made me feel that was okay too. Jessie Koester: You guided my writing efforts and {drum roll) you came up with the book title that won my heart - Down a Peg. Thank you, Jessie. Elliot Toman and Jason Smith: You guys brought my website and book into this world for all to see. You get the award for patience and legerdemain. Lovely to behold. Thank you to you both.

Peter Yagesic

You win the Maiden Voyage Award. My first steps toward sorting, linking and codifying my Art in Real Life thoughts into a website happened with you. You got me onto the starting line. Thank you.

To all my family and friends:

You must have often wondered if I would ever actually birth this baby but you stayed the course with me. You gave me strength and gave me room. Thank you to you all. Now I promise to move on and talk about something else. Well, that's not exactly true. Maybe I'll dial down the frequency. Thank you to everyone.

ABOUT THE AUTHOR

While you were watching the performance, Susan was probably watching you. Forever curious about the power of the arts to inspire, change and unite us, she turned that interest into a career - helping organizations such as LL.Bean, Chase Bank and Blue Man Group safely navigate through large-scale change.

In Down a Peg Susan now brings the arts into the foreground of your own life, offering a playful mix of personal experiences, brain science and cultural history. She lives in Philadelphia happily dreaming up paper mache projects.

You can visit her online at **ArtInRealLife.com**.